COOK'S KITCHEN

Gluten Free

igloobooks

Published in 2015
by Igloo Books Ltd
Cottage Farm
Sywell
NN6 0BJ
www.igloobooks.com

Food photography and recipe development © Stockfood, The Food Media Agency
Cover images © Stockfood, The Food Media Agency

HUN001 0715
2 4 6 8 10 9 7 5 3 1
ISBN: 978-1-78440-824-4

Printed and manufactured in China

Contents

Breakfasts

Poached Egg with Potato Pancake

SERVES 4

PREPARATION TIME 15 MINUTES

COOKING TIME 30 MINUTES

INGREDIENTS

750 g / 1 lb 10 oz / 3 cups white potatoes,
   peeled and diced
2 tbsp unsalted butter
1 onion, finely chopped
2 spring onions (scallions), chopped
75 g / 3 oz / ½ cup cornflour (cornstarch)
2 tbsp sunflower oil
2 tbsp white wine vinegar
4 large eggs
55 g / 2 oz / 1 cup rocket (arugula)
a small handful of cress
salt and freshly ground black pepper

METHOD

- Cook the potatoes in a large saucepan of salted, boiling water for 15–18 minutes until tender.

- Meanwhile, melt the butter in a frying pan set over a medium heat until hot. Add the onion, spring onion and a little salt, sweating for 6–7 minutes until softened.

- Drain the potatoes and leave them to steam dry for a few minutes. Mash well, incorporating the sweated onion mixture.

- Season to taste, divide the mixture into four and shape into thick pancakes. Dust with cornflour, shaking off the excess.

- Heat the sunflower oil in a large frying pan set over a medium heat until hot.

- Place the pancakes in the hot oil and fry for 2–3 minutes on both sides until golden and crisp.

- Heat a large saucepan of water until simmering and stir through the white wine vinegar.

- Crack the eggs into cups and slide into the water, poaching them for 3 minutes.

- Remove with a slotted spoon and drain on kitchen paper.

- Position the pancakes on plates and sit the poached eggs on top. Season with salt and pepper and garnish with rocket and cress.

TOP TIP
Trim the whites of the poached eggs with kitchen scissors for presentation.

Omelette with Avocado and Spinach

SERVES 4

PREPARATION TIME 15 MINUTES

COOKING TIME 20 MINUTES

INGREDIENTS

small eggs

g / 2 oz / ¼ cup unsalted butter

medium avocados, pitted and sliced

g / 3 ½ oz / 1 cup feta, thinly sliced

g / 3 ½ oz / 2 cups baby spinach, washed

g / 10 ½ oz / 2 cups cherry tomatoes on the vine

small bunch of chives, snipped

and freshly ground black pepper

METHOD

- Whisk together three eggs in a mixing bowl. Season with salt and pepper.

- Heat 1 tbsp of butter in an omelette or small frying pan set over a moderate heat until hot.

- Add the beaten egg to the pan, tilting it to cover the surface of the pan.

- Leave the egg to set slightly, then draw the edges inwards from the perimeter, letting the uncooked egg run under.

- Add slices of avocado and feta on top, followed by a small handful of spinach. Flip the omelette over to cover the spinach.

- Cover the pan with a lid and leave for 1 minute. Remove the lid and sprinkle over some chopped chives.

- Slide onto a plate and serve with cherry tomatoes on the side.

- Repeat the process for the remaining omelettes, using a fresh tablespoon of butter for each. Serve immediately for best results.

TOP TIP
Wash the spinach thoroughly to get rid of any dirt and grit.

Baked Eggs

METHOD

- Preheat the oven to 180°C (160°C fan) / 350F / gas 4. Grease four ramekins with half of the olive oil.

- Heat the remaining oil with the butter in a frying pan set over a moderate heat. Add the mushrooms and a pinch of salt, then fry for 4–5 minutes until tender.

- Beat four of the eggs with the milk in a mixing jug and season with salt and pepper.

- Fill the ramekins with the fried mushrooms and pour the beaten egg over them. Crack an egg into each ramekin and arrange the ramekins on a baking tray.

- Top the eggs with Gruyère and bake for 10–12 minutes until the eggs are set.

- Remove from the oven and garnish with a pinch of paprika and a sprig of oregano before serving.

SERVES 4

PREPARATION TIME 15 MINUTES

COOKING TIME 20 MINUTES

INGREDIENTS

2 tbsp olive oil
1 tbsp unsalted butter
150 g / 5 oz / 2 cups mixed mushrooms,
    brushed clean and chopped
8 large eggs
250 ml / 9 fl. oz / 1 cup whole milk
100 g / 3 ½ oz / 1 cup Gruyère, grated
½ tsp paprika
a few sprigs of oregano
salt and freshly ground black pepper

TOP TIP
Use the freshest eggs possible for this recipe.

Bacon and Egg Kedgeree

SERVES 4

PREPARATION TIME 15 MINUTES

COOKING TIME 35 MINUTES

INGREDIENTS

- 1 tbsp unsalted butter
- 1 onion, finely chopped
- 4 rashers back bacon, chopped
- 1 tsp Madras curry powder
- 175 g / 6 oz / 1 cup basmati rice, rinsed in several changes of water
- 350 ml / 12 fl. oz / 1 ½ cups vegetable stock, hot
- 4 medium eggs
- 1 small bunch of flat-leaf parsley
- salt and freshly ground black pepper

METHOD

- Melt the butter in a large saucepan or casserole dish set over a medium heat until hot.

- Add the onion, bacon and a little salt, then sweat for 5 minutes until the onion is softened.

- Sprinkle over the curry powder, stir well, and cook for a further minute. Stir in the rice and cover with the stock.

- Increase the heat and cook until the stock is boiling. Reduce the heat and cover with a lid, then cook for 15–20 minutes until the rice is tender.

- Meanwhile, cook the eggs in a saucepan of boiling water for 8 minutes. Drain and refresh in iced water immediately.

- Peel and set to one side. Roughly chop most of the parsley, reserving a few sprigs for a garnish.

- Once the rice has absorbed the stock, remove the saucepan from the heat and leave it covered for 5 minutes.

- Fluff the rice with a fork and spoon into bowls. Slice the eggs and sit on top of the rice, garnishing with a sprinkle of chopped parsley and a sprig as well.

TOP TIP
You can rinse the rice in warm water rather than several changes of cold water.

Hash Browns with Salmon and Crème Fraiche

SERVES 4

PREPARATION TIME 20 MINUTES

COOKING TIME 25 MINUTES

INGREDIENTS

1 kg / 2 lb 2 oz / 6 ⅔ cups Desiree potatoes, peeled
1 onion, finely chopped
2 tbsp sunflower oil
2 tbsp unsalted butter
350 g / 12 oz / 1 ½ cups crème fraiche
300 g / 10 ½ oz / 2 cups cooked salmon, flaked
a small bunch of chives, snipped
1 lemon
flaked sea salt and freshly ground black pepper

METHOD

- Preheat the oven to 140°C (120°C fan) / 275F / gas 1. Roughly grate the potatoes and dry them well using a clean tea towel.

- Once dried, place in a bowl and add the onion and seasoning, stirring well.

- Heat together 1 tbsp of oil and butter in a large frying pan set over a medium heat until hot.

- Drop generous tablespoons of the potato mixture into the pan, placed in mounds and spaced apart. Gently flatten the mounds using a spatula or fish slice and cook for 5–7 minutes until browned underneath.

- Flip and cook the other side for 4–5 minutes until lightly browned. Remove to a plate that is lined with greaseproof paper and keep warm in the oven.

- Add the remaining butter and oil to the pan and cook the remaining potato mixture in the same way.

- Top the hash browns with crème fraiche, flaked salmon, and chives. Grate over some fresh lemon zest and sprinkle with salt and freshly ground pepper. Serve with the remaining crème fraiche on the side.

TOP TIP
Try slices of smoked ham instead of salmon when next preparing this recipe.

Pancakes

INGREDIENTS

110 g / 4 oz / ⅔ cup chestnut flour
1 tbsp gluten-free plain (all-purpose) flour
pinch of salt
½ tsp gluten-free baking powder
1 tbsp caster (superfine) sugar
2 medium eggs, beaten
250 ml / 9 fl. oz / 1 cup whole milk
55 g / 2 oz / ¼ cup unsalted butter, melted
110 g / 4 oz / ½ cup maple syrup
150 g / 5 oz / 1 cup blueberries

METHOD

- Sift together both of the flours, salt, baking powder and sugar into a large mixing bowl.

- Beat in the eggs, then gradually whisk in the milk until a batter comes together.

- Whisk in 1 tbsp of melted butter.

- Heat a large frying pan over a medium heat until hot, then grease with a little of the remaining melted butter.

- Add small ladles of the batter and let them spread out a little and set underneath. Flip the pancakes and cook for a further minute until golden on both sides.

- Slide onto a plate and keep warm to one side. Repeat the method for the remaining pancakes.

- Stack on plates and top with maple syrup and blueberries before serving.

TOP TIP

Look for small bubbles to form on the surface of the pancakes before flipping them.

19

Berry Compote

SERVES 4

PREPARATION TIME 1 HOUR 10 MINUTES

COOKING TIME 10 MINUTES

INGREDIENTS

150 g / 5 oz / 1 cup strawberries, hulled and
   chopped

125 g / 4 ½ oz / 1 cup raspberries

110 g / 4 oz / ⅔ cup blueberries

75 g / 3 oz / ⅓ cup caster (superfine) sugar

½ lemon, juiced

a small handful of blackcurrants

400 g / 14 oz / 2 cups Greek yoghurt

METHOD

- Combine the strawberries, raspberries, blueberries, sugar, lemon juice and 2 tbsp of water in a saucepan.

- Cook over a medium heat, stirring occasionally, until the sugar has dissolved and the fruit is soft and juicy.

- Continue to cook for a few minutes, stirring frequently, until the compote breaks down.

- Remove from the heat and leave it cool slightly. Cover and chill for 1 hour.

- Spoon the Greek yoghurt into small serving glasses.

- Top with the berry compote and a garnish of blackcurrants before serving.

TOP TIP
Use coconut milk yoghurt for a dairy-free version.

Tropical Fruit Salad

METHOD

- Toss together the fruit in a large mixing bowl.
- Divide between bowls and top with the Greek yoghurt and honey.
- Garnish with a sprinkle of muesli before serving.

SERVES 4
PREPARATION TIME 20 MINUTES

INGREDIENTS

150 g / 5 oz / 1 cup strawberries, hulled and chopped
150 g / 5 oz / 1 ⅓ cups raspberries
1 large orange, peeled and segmented
2 kiwi fruit, peeled and sliced
100 g / 3 ½ oz / ⅔ cup blueberries
150 g / 5 oz / 1 cup white seedless grapes, halved
75 g / 3 oz / ½ cup blackberries
225 g / 8 oz / 1 cup Greek yoghurt
75 g / 3 oz / ⅓ cup honey
4 tbsp muesli

TOP TIP

Let the fruit salad stand for 15 minutes before serving.

Roasted Stone Fruits

SERVES 4

PREPARATION TIME 15 MINUTES

COOKING TIME 45 MINUTES

INGREDIENTS

225 ml / 8 fl. oz / 1 cup water
110 g / 4 oz / ⅔ cup soft light brown sugar
1 tsp vanilla extract
a pinch ground cinnamon
3 nectarines, halved and pitted
6 star anise

METHOD

- Preheat the oven to 180°C (160°C fan) / 350F / gas 4.
- Combine the water, sugar, vanilla extract and cinnamon in a saucepan.
- Cook over a medium heat, stirring occasionally, until the sugar has completely dissolved.
- Stud the nectarine halves with star anise and arrange, cut-side facing up, in a baking dish.
- Pour over the syrup and roast the fruit for 40–45 minutes until tender to the point of a knife.
- Remove from the oven and leave to stand for 5 minutes before serving.

TOP TIP
This recipe works equally well with peaches.

Apricot Flapjacks

AKES 12

EPARATION TIME 10 MINUTES

OKING TIME 45 MINUTES

GREDIENTS

0 g / 5 oz / ⅔ cup unsalted butter, cubed
5 g / 4 ½ oz / ⅓ cup golden syrup
0 g / 9 oz / 2 cups gluten-free rolled oats
0 g / 5 oz / 1 cup dried apricots, chopped
inch of salt

METHOD

- Preheat the oven to 180°C (160°C fan) / 350F / gas 4. Grease and line an 18 cm (7 in) square baking tin with greaseproof paper.

- Melt the butter and syrup together in a large saucepan until runny. Remove from the heat and stir through the oats, chopped apricots and salt.

- Tip the mixture into the baking tray, then press down and smooth with the back of a tablespoon. Bake for 35–40 minutes until golden brown and set.

- Remove to a wire rack to cool before turning out, slicing, and serving.

TOP TIP

For best results, let the flapjack cool completely before turning out and slicing.

Summer Berry Smoothie

METHOD

- Combine the mixed berries, milk, agave nectar and oats in a large food processor or blender.
- Blitz for 2 minutes until smooth.
- Pour into glasses or bottles and serve with straws.

SERVES 4

PREPARATION TIME 5 MINUTES

INGREDIENTS

450 g / 1 lb / 2 ½ cups frozen mixed berries
500 ml / 18 fl. oz / 2 cups semi-skimmed milk
2 tbsp light agave nectar
2 tbsp gluten-free rolled oats

TOP TIP
Add more or less of the agave nectar to control the sweetness.

Banana Smoothie

METHOD

- Combine all the ingredients in a large food processor or blender.
- Blend for 2–3 minutes until smooth.
- Pour into glasses and serve immediately.

RVES 4
EPARATION TIME 10 MINUTES

GREDIENTS

1 pint 16 fl. oz / 4 cups semi-skimmed milk
rge bananas, chopped
g / 4 ½ oz / ¾ cup strawberries, hulled
and chopped
sp vanilla extract
sp light agave nectar

TOP TIP
Ice-cold milk gives the best results when making this recipe.

Soups, Salads and Lunches

Roasted Tomato and Pepper Soup

SERVES 4

PREPARATION TIME 20 MINUTES

COOKING TIME 40 MINUTES

INGREDIENTS

2 large red peppers
2 tbsp olive oil
2 shallots, finely chopped
2 cloves of garlic, minced
300 g / 10 ½ oz / 2 cups vine tomatoes, cored and diced
750 ml / 1 pint 6 fl. oz / 3 cups vegetable stock
a bunch of thyme
55 ml / 2 fl. oz / ¼ cup double (heavy) cream
salt and freshly ground black pepper

METHOD

- Preheat the grill to hot. Place the peppers on a grilling tray and roast under the grill, turning occasionally, until blistered and blackened.

- Remove from the grill and place in a plastic bag, tying securely. Leave to cool for 10 minutes.

- Remove the peppers and peel away the skin and seeds. Chop the flesh and set to one side.

- Heat the oil in a large saucepan set over a medium heat until hot. Add the shallots, garlic and a little salt, then sweat for 4–5 minutes until softened.

- Add the red pepper flesh and tomatoes. Stir well and cover with the stock, tucking the thyme into the saucepan at the same time.

- Cook at a steady simmer for 15 minutes. Remove the thyme and blend the soup with a stick blender until smooth.

- Return to a simmer and stir through the cream, seasoning to the soup to taste before serving.

TOP TIP
Make sure that the plastic bags are tied air-tight for best results.

Butternut Squash Soup

SERVES 4

PREPARATION TIME 15 MINUTES

COOKING TIME 35 MINUTES

INGREDIENTS

tbsp olive oil

tbsp unsalted butter

large onion, finely chopped

stalk of celery, peeled and chopped

50 g / 1 lb 10 oz / 3 cups butternut squash,
peeled and diced

tsp thyme, chopped

50 ml / 1pint 6 fl. oz / 3 cups vegetable stock

5 g / 3 oz / ⅓ cup crème fraiche

tbsp flat-leaf parsley

alt and freshly ground black pepper

METHOD

- Heat together the oil and butter in a large saucepan set over a medium heat until hot.

- Add the onion, celery, butternut squash and a little salt. Sweat for 7–8 minutes until softened.

- Stir in the thyme and cover the vegetables with the stock. Heat the soup until simmering. Cook steadily for 20 minutes.

- Blend until smooth using a stick blender, then season to taste with salt and pepper.

- Ladle into serving bowls and garnish with a swirl of crème fraiche, some parsley, and a little more freshly ground pepper.

TOP TIP

Cover the saucepan with a lid when cooking the butternut squash.

Mushroom Soup

SERVES 4

PREPARATION TIME 15 MINUTES

COOKING TIME 30 MINUTES

INGREDIENTS

2 tbsp olive oil

2 shallots, finely chopped

2 cloves of garlic, minced

300 g / 10 ½ oz / 4 cups closed-cup
mushrooms, brushed clean and diced

½ tsp dried thyme

750 ml / 1 pint 6 fl. oz / 3 cups vegetable stock

150 ml / 5 fl. oz / ⅔ cup double (heavy) cream

2 tbsp unsalted butter

150 g / 5 oz / 2 cups mixed wild mushrooms,
brushed clean

2 tbsp thyme sprigs

salt and freshly ground black pepper

METHOD

- Heat the oil in a large saucepan set over a medium heat until hot.

- Add the shallot, garlic, closed-cup mushrooms, dried thyme and a little salt. Sweat for 7–8 minutes, stirring occasionally.

- Cover with the stock and cook until simmering. Simmer steadily for 15 minutes.

- Stir through the cream, return the soup to a simmer, then blend with a stick blender until smooth. Season to taste and keep warm to one side.

- Melt the butter in a frying pan set over a moderate heat until hot.

- Add the mixed wild mushrooms and a little salt, then fry for 4–5 minutes until golden and tender.

- Ladle the soup into bowls and spoon in the wild mushrooms, garnishing with fresh thyme.

TOP TIP
Make sure the soup doesn't approach boiling point when keeping warm.

Cream of Broccoli Soup

RVES 4

EPARATION TIME 15 MINUTES

OKING TIME 30 MINUTES

GREDIENTS

bsp olive oil

arge onion, finely chopped

tick of celery, peeled and diced

mall heads of broccoli, prepared
into florets

/ 1 pint 16 fl. oz / 4 cups vegetable stock

5 ml / 8 fl. oz / 1 cup double (heavy) cream

g / 3 oz / ¾ cup flaked (slivered) almonds,
toasted

t and freshly ground black pepper

METHOD

- Heat the olive oil in a large saucepan set over a medium heat until hot.

- Add the onion, celery and a little salt. Sweat for 4–5 minutes until softened.

- Add the broccoli and cover with the stock. Cook until simmering.

- Simmer for 15–20 minutes until the broccoli is tender to the point of a knife.

- Stir through the cream, then return the soup to a simmer. Blend until smooth with a stick blender.

- Season to taste with salt and pepper.

- Ladle into bowls and garnish with flaked almonds and a little more black pepper before serving.

TOP TIP

If you don't have a stick blender, blend the soup in a food processor.

Minestrone Soup

SERVES 4

PREPARATION TIME 20 MINUTES

COOKING TIME 40 MINUTES

INGREDIENTS

3 tbsp olive oil
1 large onion, finely chopped
2 cloves of garlic, finely chopped
2 large carrots, peeled and diced
½ tsp dried oregano
½ tsp dried basil
1 large red pepper, diced
4 baby leeks, chopped
1 small white cabbage, chopped
400 g / 14 oz / 2 cups canned butter
    beans, drained
200 g / 7 oz / 1 cup canned cannellini
    beans, drained
400 g / 14 oz / 2 cups passata
1 l / 1 pint 16 fl. oz / 4 cups vegetable stock
a small bunch of flat-leaf parsley, chopped
salt and freshly ground black pepper

METHOD

- Heat the olive oil in a large saucepan or casserole dish set over a medium heat until hot.
- Add the onion, garlic, carrot, dried herbs and a little salt. Sweat for 6–7 minutes until softened.
- Add the pepper, leeks and cabbage, then continue to cook for a further 5 minutes.
- Stir in the beans and cover the vegetables with the passata and stock. Heat until simmering.
- Cook steadily for 20–25 minutes until the beans are tender.
- Stir through the parsley and season to taste with salt and pepper. Ladle into bowls and serve.

TOP TIP

Add a dash of lemon juice to cut through the soup just before serving.

Sausage and Bean Soup

RVES 4

EPARATION TIME 20 MINUTES

OKING TIME 45 MINUTES

INGREDIENTS

- sp olive oil
- g / 5 oz / 1 cup smoked ham, diced
-) g / 9 oz / 1 ⅔ cups gluten-free smoked sausage, sliced
- mall leek, sliced
- rge onion, chopped
- rge carrots, peeled and sliced
- aby turnips, peeled and sliced
-) g / 14 oz / 2 cups canned cannellini beans, drained
-) g / 7 oz / 1 cup canned butter beans, drained
- 5 l / 2 pints 4 fl. oz / 5 cups vegetable stock
- mall bunch of flat-leaf parsley, chopped
- and freshly ground black pepper

METHOD

- Heat the olive oil in a large saucepan set over a medium heat until hot.
- Add the smoked ham and sausage, then fry gently for 4–5 minutes until lightly browned.
- Add the leek, onion, carrot and turnip to the saucepan. Stir well, cooking for a further 5–6 minutes until softened.
- Stir through the beans and cover with the stock.
- Simmer, then cook over a reduced heat for 25–30 minutes until the beans are tender.
- Season to taste with salt and pepper. Ladle into bowls and garnish with a sprinkle of chopped parsley.

TOP TIP
Substitute the meat for halved new potatoes to make a vegetarian version.

Chicken Noodle Soup

SERVES 4

PREPARATION TIME 10 MINUTES

COOKING TIME 20 MINUTES

INGREDIENTS

2 tbsp groundnut oil

2 large skinless chicken breasts, sliced

225 g / 8 oz / 2 cups baby sweetcorn, split
   in half

1 l / 1 pint 16 fl. oz / 4 cups chicken stock

250 ml / 9 fl. oz / 1 cup coconut milk

225 g / 8 oz / 2 cups rice noodles

2 tbsp rice wine vinegar

2 tbsp fish sauce

1 tbsp light soy sauce

a small bunch of coriander (cilantro),
   roughly chopped

1 red chilli (chili) pepper, seeded and
   finely chopped

METHOD

- Heat the oil in a large saucepan set
  over a moderate heat until hot.

- Add the chicken and brown slightly
  in the hot oil for 2 minutes.

- Stir in the corn and cover with the
  stock and coconut milk, then cook
  until simmering.

- Reduce to a gentle simmer for
  5 minutes and add the noodles.

- Continue to cook for 8–10 minutes
  until the noodles are soft.

- Season to taste with rice wine
  vinegar, fish sauce and soy sauce.

- Ladle into bowls and garnish with
  coriander and chilli before serving.

TOP TIP

Experiment with
different types of
noodle for different
textures.

Mixed Bean and Feta Salad

SERVES 4

PREPARATION TIME 15 MINUTES

COOKING TIME 5 MINUTES

INGREDIENTS

400 g / 14 oz / 4 cups green (string) beans, trimmed

250 g / 9 oz / 2 cups broad (fava) beans, shelled

4 large vine tomatoes, cored and diced

100 g / 3 ½ oz / 1 cup walnuts

150 g / 5 oz / 1 ½ cups feta, cubed

90 ml / 3 fl. oz / ⅓ cup extra-virgin olive oil

50 g / 2 oz / 1 cup rocket (arugula)

Salt and freshly ground black pepper

METHOD

- Cook the green beans in a large saucepan of salted, boiling water for 2 minutes.
- Add the broad beans and cook for a further 2 minutes, then drain well and refresh immediately in iced water.
- Drain again and toss well with the tomatoes, walnuts, feta, olive oil, rocket and plenty of seasoning.
- Spoon onto a platter and serve.

TOP TIP
Prepare a bowl of iced water before starting the recipe.

Avocado and Tomato Salad

SERVES 4

PREPARATION TIME 10 MINUTES

INGREDIENTS

100 ml / 3 ½ fl. oz / ½ cup olive oil
2 tbsp lemon juice
1 tbsp honey
2 large avocados, pitted and diced
225 g / 8 oz / 1 ½ cups cherry tomatoes
150 g / 5 oz / 1 cup Kalamata olives
225 g / 8 oz / 2 cups feta, cubed
100 g / 3 ½ oz / 2 cups rocket (arugula)
salt and freshly ground black pepper

METHOD

- Whisk together the olive oil, lemon juice, honey and seasoning in a mixing bowl until smooth.
- Add the avocado, cherry tomatoes, olives, feta and rocket. Toss well to coat.
- Lift the salad into bowls and serve.

TOP TIP

Using pitted olives in this recipe is time-saving and more convenient.

Beetroot and Red Onion Salad

SERVES 4

PREPARATION TIME 15 MINUTES

COOKING TIME 50 MINUTES

INGREDIENTS

12 small beets, washed, peeled and halved
1 tbsp olive oil
1 tbsp balsamic vinegar
100 g / 3 ½ oz / 2 cups beetroot leaves
225 g / 8 oz / 2 cups feta, crumbled
1 small red onion, finely chopped
55 ml / 2 fl. oz / ¼ cup extra-virgin olive oil
salt and freshly ground black pepper

METHOD

- Preheat the oven to 200°C (180°C fan) / 400F / gas 6.
- Toss the beets with the olive oil and plenty of seasoning. Arrange on a baking tray and roast for 40–45 minutes until tender to the point of a knife.
- Remove from the oven and leave to cool.
- Toss with the balsamic vinegar, seasoning with salt and pepper at the same time.
- Arrange the beetroot leaves on serving plates and top with the dressed beets, crumbled feta and chopped red onion.
- Drizzle with extra-virgin olive oil and season with salt and pepper before serving.

TOP TIP
Try using crumbled blue cheese or goats' cheese as an alternative to feta.

Chicken and Bacon Salad

METHOD

- Preheat the grill to hot. Toss the chicken with the sunflower oil and season with salt and pepper.
- Grill for 8–10 minutes, turning once, until cooked through and golden.
- Cook the eggs in a large saucepan of boiling water for 10 minutes.
- Remove the chicken from the grill and set to one side. Drain the eggs and refresh in iced water.
- Grill the bacon for 5–6 minutes, turning once, until crisp and dark golden in appearance. Remove from the grill and drain on kitchen paper.
- Peel the eggs and cut into slices. Roughly chop the bacon and toss with the cherry tomatoes, lettuce, avocado, chicken and sliced egg.
- Spoon onto plates and top with pumpkin and sesame seeds before serving.

SERVES 4

PREPARATION TIME 15 MINUTES

COOKING TIME 20 MINUTES

INGREDIENTS

2 large chicken breasts, skinned and sliced
2 tbsp sunflower oil
4 small eggs
6 rashers streaky bacon
225 g / 8 oz / 1 ½ cups cherry tomatoes,
   halved
4 little gem lettuce, chopped
1 large avocado, pitted and diced
55 g / 2 oz / ½ cup pumpkin seeds
1 tbsp sesame seeds
salt and freshly ground black pepper

TOP TIP
Use cooked chicken breast for a quick version of this salad.

Smoked Mackerel Salad

SERVES 4

PREPARATION TIME 15 MINUTES

COOKING TIME 25 MINUTES

INGREDIENTS

small new potatoes

small courgettes (zucchinis), roughly sliced diagonally

100 g / 3 ½ oz / 2 cups mixed salad leaves, washed

bunch flat-leaf parsley, roughly chopped

sprigs of tarragon, roughly chopped

400 g / 14 oz / 2 ⅔ cups smoked mackerel, flaked

75 ml / 3 fl. oz / ⅓ cup olive oil

tbsp white wine vinegar

salt and freshly ground black pepper

METHOD

- Cook the potatoes in a large saucepan of salted, boiling water until tender; 15–18 minutes.

- Remove from the saucepan using a slotted spoon and transfer to a bowl of iced water.

- Add the courgette to the boiling water and cook for 3 minutes. Drain well and add to the bowl of iced water.

- Drain the vegetables and gently mix with the salad leaves, herbs and flaked fish.

- Briefly whisk together the oil and vinegar, then season with salt and pepper.

- Toss with the salad ingredients and lift onto plates before serving.

TOP TIP

Smoked haddock would work well as a substitute for the mackerel.

Steak Salad

METHOD

- Prepare the pesto by placing the basil, pine nuts, extra-virgin olive oil, garlic a[nd] a little salt in a food processor. Blitz unt[il] smooth, then add the Parmesan and pu[lse] until a thicker consistency is reached. Chill until needed.

- Cook the new potatoes in salted boiling water for 15–18 minutes until tender. Drain and allow to cool a little.

- Meanwhile, heat a heavy-based frying pan over a high heat until smoking. Brush the steaks with the groundnut oil and season well.

- Cook the steaks for 6 minutes, turning after 3 minutes. Transfer to a plate and keep warm, covered loosely with foil.

- Heat the olive oil and butter in a large frying pan set over a medium heat. Fry the cooked potatoes for 4–5 minutes until golden. Remove from the heat and dress with some of the pesto.

- Arrange the rocket and sun-dried tomatoes on serving plates. Slice the steaks into 2 cm (1 in) wide strips and arrange on the salad.

- Dress with some of the pesto and serve with portions of the sautéed potatoes on the side.

SERVES 4

PREPARATION TIME 15 MINUTES

COOKING TIME 30 MINUTES

INGREDIENTS

a handful of basil leaves
100 g / 3 ½ oz / 1 cup pine nuts, toasted
110 ml / 4 fl. oz / ½ cup extra-virgin olive oil
2 cloves of garlic, crushed
75 g / 3 oz / ¾ cup Parmesan, grated
300 g / 10 ½ oz / 2 cups new potatoes
2 x 180 g / 6 ½ oz sirloin steaks, trimmed
55 ml / 2 fl. oz / ¼ cup groundnut oil
55 ml / 2 fl. oz / ¼ cup olive oil
2 tbsp butter
150 g / 5 oz / 3 cups rocket (arugula)
110 g / 4 oz / ⅔ cup sun-dried tomatoes in oil, drained and chopped
salt and freshly ground black pepper

TOP TIP
Let the steaks rest for at least 10 minutes before slicing and serving in the salad.

Courgette and Green Vegetable Frittata

SERVES 4

PREPARATION TIME 15 MINUTES

COOKING TIME 35 MINUTES

INGREDIENTS

- tbsp olive oil
- large leek, chopped
- large courgettes (zucchinis), sliced
- g / 8 oz / 2 cups asparagus, trimmed with woody ends removed
- g / 5 oz / 1 ½ cups petit pois
- small bunch of chervil, chopped
- medium eggs, beaten
- / 3 oz / ¾ cup Cheddar, grated
- Salt and freshly ground black pepper

METHOD

- Preheat the oven to 180°C (160°C fan) / 350F / gas 4.
- Heat the oil in a cast-iron frying pan set over a moderate heat until hot.
- Add the leek and courgette, then fry for 4–5 minutes until lightly golden.
- Add the asparagus, peas and chervil. Stir, then cover with the beaten egg.
- Season with salt and pepper, then sprinkle over the grated Cheddar.
- Bake for 20–25 minutes until golden on top and set.
- Remove from the oven and leave to stand for 5 minutes before serving.

TOP TIP
You can use fresh or frozen petit pois in this recipe.

Crispy Crab Cakes

METHOD

- Whisk together the yoghurt, mayonna half the paprika and some seasoning i small mixing bowl.
- Squeeze the juice from half a lemon in the mixture and stir briefly. Cover and chill until ready to serve.
- Tip the crab into a bowl and add the ch egg white, cornflour, remaining paprik Cayenne and some seasoning.
- Mix thoroughly until combined. Shape mixture into cakes and arrange on a tr
- Heat tablespoons of the oil in a large fr pan set over a medium heat until hot.
- Season the cakes and fry for 5–6 minut turning once, until golden on both side
- Serve immediately with the sauce, a sprinkling of chopped parsley and the remaining lemon.

SERVES 4

PREPARATION TIME 15 MINUTES

COOKING TIME 15—20 MINUTES

INGREDIENTS

250 g / 9 oz / 1 cup plain yoghurt
110 g / 4 oz / ½ cup mayonnaise
1 tsp paprika
1 lemon, halved
450 g / 1 lb / 3 cups crab meat, picked through
    for shell
1 red chilli (chili), seeded and
    finely chopped
1 small egg white, lightly beaten
2 tbsp cornflour (cornstarch)
a pinch of Cayenne
55 ml / 2 fl. oz / ¼ cup sunflower oil
a small bunch of flat-leaf parsley,
    roughly chopped
salt and freshly ground black pepper

TOP TIP
A fish slice is perfect when it comes to flipping the crab cakes in the pan.

Spring Rolls

KES 8

PARATION TIME 20 MINUTES

KING TIME 5 MINUTES

REDIENTS

g / 3 ½ oz / 1 cup rice vermicelli noodles

ring roll rice wrappers

sp Thai basil, chopped

sp mint, chopped

sp coriander (cilantro)

lettuce leaves

ndfuls bean sprouts

tbsp fish sauce

nl / 3 fl. oz / ⅓ cup warm water

sp lime juice

d chilli (chili), seeded and finely diced

oves of garlic, minced

sp caster (superfine) sugar

METHOD

- Cook the rice vermicelli in a saucepan of salted, boiling water for 3–5 minutes, until 'al dente'. Drain well and rinse thoroughly with cold water to prevent sticking.

- Fill a large bowl with warm water. Dip a wrapper into the water to soften and lay it flat.

- In a row across the centre, place a small handful of noodles, basil, mint, coriander, lettuce and bean sprouts, leaving about 5 cm (2 in) uncovered on each side.

- Fold the uncovered sides inward and tightly roll the wrapper, starting at the end with the lettuce.

- Repeat the process with the remaining filling ingredients.

- Mix together the dipping sauce ingredients in a small serving bowl, making sure that the sugar has dissolved. Serve with the spring rolls.

TOP TIP
Keep the noodles in cold water after rinsing to ensure they remain separated.

Hummus and Pitta Bread

SERVES 4

PREPARATION TIME 10 MINUTES

COOKING TIME 5 MINUTES

INGREDIENTS

600 g / 1 lb 5 oz / 3 cups canned chickpeas
(garbanzo beans), drained
150 ml / 5 fl. oz / ⅔ cup water
2 cloves of garlic, minced
2 tbsp tahini paste
1 tsp ground cumin
2 tbsp lemon juice
1 tsp smoked paprika
55 ml / 2 fl. oz / ¼ cup extra-virgin olive oil
4 white gluten-free pitta breads
salt and freshly ground black pepper

METHOD

- Combine the chickpeas with the water, garlic, tahini, cumin, lemon juice and ½ tsp of smoked paprika in a food processor.
- Blitz until smooth, then add 2 tbsp of olive oil once the mixture starts to break up and become smooth.
- Continue to blitz until smooth. Season to taste with salt and pepper.
- Spoon into a serving bowl and garnish with the remaining olive oil and paprika.
- Toast the pitta breads under a hot grill before serving with the hummus.

TOP TIP

Top the hummus with a dollop of basil pesto.

Pasta and Grains

Lasagne

SERVES 8

PREPARATION TIME 1 HOUR 20 MINUTES

COOKING TIME 1 HOUR

INGREDIENTS

2 tbsp olive oil
1 onion, finely chopped
1 green pepper, diced
2 cloves of garlic, minced
500 g / 1 lb 2 oz / 3 ⅓ cups beef mince
400 g / 14 oz / 2 cups canned chopped
    tomatoes
150 ml / 5 fl. oz / ⅔ cup red wine
250 ml / 9 fl. oz / 1 cup beef stock
2 tbsp unsalted butter, plus extra for greasing
2 tbsp cornflour (cornstarch)
500 ml / 18 fl. oz / 2 cups whole milk
a pinch of ground nutmeg
400 g / 14 oz / 4 cups gluten-free lasagne
    sheets
100 g / 3 ½ oz / 1 cup Parmesan, grated
100 g / 3 ½ oz / ⅔ cup cherry tomatoes on
    the vine
salt and freshly ground black pepper

METHOD

- Heat the oil in a large casserole dish set over a medium heat. Sweat the chopped vegetables for 6–8 minutes. Add the garlic and cook for 2 minutes. Increase the heat and add the mince, browning well all over.

- Once browned, cover with the chopped tomatoes, red wine and stock. Increase the heat and cook until simmering, then reduce the heat to low and cook for 1 hour. Adjust the seasoning to taste and set to one side.

- Melt the butter in a saucepan set over a moderate heat, then whisk in the flour to make a roux, cooking until golden.

- Whisk in the milk in a slow, steady stream until a sauce forms. Simmer for 5 minutes and season to taste.

- Preheat the oven to 180°C (160°C fan) / 350F / gas 4 and grease a large rectangular baking dish with a little butter.

- Spread a little white sauce over the base, then top with a layer of lasagne sheets, some meat sauce, more white sauce and a layer of lasagne sheets. Repeat the process again, finishing with a layer of white sauce. Sprinkle over the Parmesan and sit the cherry tomatoes on the vine on top.

- Bake for 1 hour until golden on top and piping hot throughout before serving.

TOP TIP
Substitute the chopped tomatoes for passata for a smoother meat sauce.

Bolognese Tagliatelle

SERVES 4

PREPARATION TIME 15 MINUTES

COOKING TIME 1 HOUR

INGREDIENTS

1 tbsp olive oil

1 onion, finely chopped

2 cloves of garlic, minced

150 g / 5 oz / 1 cup cherry tomatoes

450 g / 1 lb / 3 cups beef mince

100 ml / 3 ½ fl. oz / ½ cup red wine

250 ml / 9 fl. oz / 1 cup beef stock

400 g / 14 oz / 2 cups passata

1 small bunch of basil

400 g / 14 oz / 4 cups gluten-free tagliatelle

55 g / 2 oz / ½ cup Parmesan, grated

Salt and freshly ground black pepper

METHOD

- Heat the olive oil in a casserole dish set over a medium heat until hot.

- Add the onion, garlic, cherry tomatoes and a little salt, then sweat for 5–6 minutes until softened.

- Increase the heat slightly and add the mince, browning well all over.

- Add the red wine and deglaze the dish, stirring and scraping the base with a spoon. Cover with the beef stock and passata.

- Bring the sauce to a simmer, then cook over a reduced heat for 40–45 minutes, stirring occasionally.

- Season to taste with salt and pepper, then keep warm to one side.

- Cook the tagliatelle in a large saucepan of salted, boiling water until 'al dente'; 8–10 minutes.

- Drain well and toss with some of the sauce. Lift into bowls and top with more sauce, grated Parmesan and a sprig of basil before serving.

TOP TIP

Stir 1 tbsp of soft butter into the sauce for a luxurious finish.

Spicy Chorizo Pasta

SERVES 4

PREPARATION TIME 10 MINUTES

COOKING TIME 10 MINUTES

INGREDIENTS

400 g / 14 oz / 4 cups gluten-free pasta

1 tbsp olive oil

300 g / 10 ½ oz / link of chorizo, peeled
    and sliced

1 clove of garlic, minced

1 tsp dried red chilli (chili) flakes

75 g / 3 oz / ⅓ cup sun-dried tomatoes in oil,
    drained and chopped

300 g / 10 ½ oz / 1 ½ cups passata

a pinch of caster (superfine) sugar

a small bunch of flat-leaf parsley, chopped

salt and freshly ground black pepper

METHOD

- Cook the pasta in a large saucepan of salted, boiling water for 8–10 minutes until 'al dente'.

- Meanwhile, heat the oil in a large saucepan over a moderate heat until hot. Add the chorizo and fry for 4–5 minutes until golden.

- Add the garlic and fry for 30 seconds, stirring, then add the chilli flakes, sun-dried tomato, passata and sugar.

- Stir well and simmer over a reduced heat for 5 minutes. Season to taste.

- Drain the pasta well and toss immediate in the tomato sauce. Stir through the parsley and spoon into bowls before servi

TOP TIP
Any kind of cured meat, such as salami, works well in this recipe.

Easy Tomato Pasta

SERVES 4

PREPARATION TIME 10 MINUTES

COOKING TIME 10 MINUTES

INGREDIENTS

400 g / 14 oz / 4 cups gluten-free fusilli

2 tbsp olive oil

1 clove of garlic, minced

400 g / 14 oz / 2 cups canned
chopped tomatoes

1 pinch of caster (superfine) sugar

2 tbsp basil leaves

Salt and freshly ground black pepper

METHOD

- Cook the fusilli in a large saucepan of salted, boiling water until 'al dente'; 8–10 minutes.

- Meanwhile, heat the oil in a large saucepan set over a medium heat until hot. Add the garlic and fry gently for 1 minute.

- Add the chopped tomatoes and sugar. Stir well and simmer for 5 minutes until slightly thickened.

- Season the sauce with salt and pepper and keep warm to one side.

- Drain the pasta and toss immediately in the sauce. Season to taste with salt and pepper.

- Divide between bowls and garnish with basil leaves before serving.

TOP TIP

Try adding a pinch of chilli (chili) flakes for a kick.

Lemon and Asparagus Pasta

SERVES 4

PREPARATION TIME 10 MINUTES

COOKING TIME 15 MINUTES

INGREDIENTS

1 lemon

350 g / 12 oz / 3 ½ cups gluten-free penne

1 tbsp olive oil

150 g / 5 oz / 1 cup pancetta lardons

110 g / 4 oz / ⅔ cup cherry tomatoes, halved

225 g / 8 oz / 2 cups asparagus, woody ends removed

a bunch of basil, leaves picked

a small bunch of flat-leaf parsley, chopped

75 g / 3 oz / ¾ cup Parmesan, shaved

salt and freshly ground black pepper

METHOD

- Juice and zest the lemon, then set to one side.

- Cook the penne in a large saucepan of salted, boiling water until 'al dente'; around 8–10 minutes.

- Meanwhile, heat the olive oil in a large saucepan set over a medium heat until ▌ Add the pancetta and fry for 4 minutes until golden.

- Add the cherry tomatoes and asparagus cooking for 4–5 minutes until softened.

- Drain the penne when ready and add to the pancetta and vegetables. Toss wel then add the basil, parsley, lemon zest a juice at the same time.

- Stir through the Parmesan and season to taste.

- Spoon onto a platter before serving.

TOP TIP

If needed, add a little cooking water to the pasta when tossing to prevent sticking.

Thai Chicken Stir-fry

RVES 4

EPARATION TIME 10 MINUTES

OKING TIME 15 MINUTES

GREDIENTS

bsp vegetable oil
oneless skinless chicken breasts, sliced
ed onion, sliced
bsp ginger, peeled and finely sliced
tick of lemon grass, finely sliced
loves of garlic, finely sliced
aby leek, finely sliced
ushrooms, sliced
arrots, finely sliced
ourgette (zucchini), chopped
mall cabbage, finely sliced
bsp almonds
ed pepper, 1 green pepper, 1 yellow pepper,
seeds removed, finely sliced
bsp cornflour (cornstarch), mixed with a
little water
ml / 2 fl. oz / ¼ cup tamari sauce
ml / 2 fl. oz / ¼ cup rice wine
bsp sesame oil
bsp white sesame seeds
bsp black sesame seeds
4 spring onions (scallions), thinly sliced
lengthwise
andful Thai basil leaves

METHOD

- Heat a large wok over a high heat,
  then add 1 tbsp of oil and stir-fry
  half the chicken for 3 minutes, until
  cooked through. Transfer to a bowl
  and repeat with the remaining
  chicken, then set aside.

- Heat the remaining oil in the wok
  and add the onion, ginger, lemon
  grass, garlic and leek. Stir-fry for
  2 minutes.

- Add the mushrooms, carrots,
  courgettes, cabbage, almonds and
  peppers and stir-fry for 2 minutes.

- Add the chicken along with the
  juices, then add the cornflour, tamari
  sauce, rice wine and sesame oil.
  Stir-fry for a further 2–3 minutes.

- Put onto serving plates and sprinkle
  with sesame seeds. Garnish with
  sliced spring onions and Thai basil.

TOP TIP

Stir and toss the
vegetables to keep them
moving around the pan
to cook evenly.

Mushroom Risotto

SERVES 4

PREPARATION TIME 15 MINUTES

COOKING TIME 50 MINUTES

INGREDIENTS

2 tbsp olive oil
2 tbsp unsalted butter
1 shallot, finely chopped
2 cloves of garlic, minced
150 g / 5 oz / 2 cups oyster mushrooms,
    brushed clean and roughly chopped
100 g / 3 ½ oz / ⅔ cup sun-dried tomatoes,
    soaked in hot water for 10 minutes
200 g / 7 oz / 1 cup Arborio rice
110 ml / 4 fl. oz / ½ cup dry white wine
1.2 l / 2 pints 2 fl. oz / 5 cups vegetable stock,
    kept hot on the stove
55 g / 2 oz / ¼ cup Parmesan, finely grated
2 tbsp sage
salt and freshly ground black pepper

METHOD

- Heat together the oil and butter in a larg
  saucepan set over a medium heat until h
- Add the shallot, garlic and mushrooms.
  Fry gently for 5–6 minutes until softene
- Drain the tomatoes and roughly chop.
  Add to the saucepan, stirring well.
- Add the rice and stir well to coat in the o
  and butter. Cook for 3–4 minutes until th
  grains start to turn translucent.
- Deglaze the saucepan with the wine,
  increasing the heat to allow it to evapora
  almost entirely.
- Add the hot vegetable stock to the risott
  a ladle at a time, stirring frequently unti
  each ladle has been absorbed.
- Continue in this fashion until all the sto
  has been absorbed and the rice is soft ye
  still has some bite; 30–35 minutes.
- Stir through the Parmesan and season th
  risotto with salt and pepper. Serve with
  garnish of sage.

TOP TIP

If you run out of stock,
use hot water to finish
cooking the risotto.

Seafood Paella

SERVES 4

PREPARATION TIME 15 MINUTES

COOKING TIME 45 MINUTES

INGREDIENTS

60 ml / 2 fl. oz / ¼ cup olive oil

1 large onion, chopped

2 cloves of garlic, minced

1 yellow pepper, sliced

150 g / 5 oz / 1 cup chorizo, peeled and diced

300 g / 10 ½ oz / 1 ½ cups paella rice

1 pinch of saffron threads

1.5 l / 2 pints 4 fl. oz / 5 cups chicken stock

1 tsp smoked paprika

200 g / 5 oz / 1 ½ cups petit pois

500 g / 1 lb / 3 cups prawns (shrimps), peeled and deveined

1 lemon, juiced

Salt and freshly ground black pepper

METHOD

- Heat the olive oil in a large, shallow pan and cook the onion, garlic and pepper for 6–7 minutes until soft.

- Add the chorizo and cook for a further 5 minutes, stirring occasionally. Stir in the paella rice and coat thoroughly in the oil.

- Stir the saffron into the stock and pour the infused stock over the rice.

- Add the paprika, stir well, and cook until simmering. Leave to cook steadily, uncovered, for 20 minutes until the rice is almost tender.

- Add the peas and prawns and cook for a further 8–10 minutes, stirring occasionally, until the prawns are tender and cooked through.

- Stir through the lemon juice and season with salt and pepper before serving.

TOP TIP
If you can't find paella rice, use white short-grain as an alternative.

85

Egg-fried Rice

METHOD

- Combine the rice with 600 ml / 1 pt 2 fl [oz] / 2 ½ cups of slightly salted water in a la[rge] saucepan. Cook over a moderate heat until boiling.

- Cover and cook over a very low heat for 20–25 minutes, until the water has been absorbed. Remove from the heat and le[ave] to cool, covered, to one side.

- Lightly whisk the eggs with the sesame [oil] and a little salt.

- Heat the groundnut oil in a wok and stir-fry the cold rice for 3 minutes.

- Add the beaten eggs and stir-fry for a further 2–3 minutes.

- Season with salt and pepper, add the spring onions and stir-fry for a further 2 minutes.

- Spoon into bowls and serve immediate[ly]

SERVES 4

PREPARATION TIME 10 MINUTES

COOKING TIME 35 MINUTES

INGREDIENTS

300 g / 10 ½ oz / 1 ⅔ cups long-grain rice,
    rinsed in several changes of water
2 large eggs
1 tbsp sesame oil
2 tbsp groundnut oil
2 spring onions (scallions), finely chopped
salt and freshly ground black pepper

TOP TIP

Before frying, let the rice cool as much as possible for best results.

Curried Vegetable Rice

RVES 4

EPARATION TIME 10 MINUTES

OKING TIME 10 MINUTES

GREDIENTS

bsp sunflower oil

sp cumin seeds

tsp coriander seeds

nion, finely sliced

reen pepper, finely diced

sp ground turmeric

0 g / 7 oz / 1 cup canned red kidney beans, drained

0 g / 12 oz / 3 cups cooked pilau rice

t and freshly ground black pepper

METHOD

- Heat the oil in a large, deep-sided sauté pan or wok set over a moderate heat until hot.

- Add the cumin and coriander seeds and leave them to pop. Add the onion and green pepper.

- Sauté for 3–4 minutes until lightly coloured, then stir in the turmeric and kidney beans.

- Cook for 30 seconds and add the rice. Stir well and sauté for a further 4–5 minutes over a reduced heat until the rice is piping hot.

- Season to taste before spooning into serving dishes.

TOP TIP

Day-old rice is perfect in this recipe.

Quinoa Tabbouleh

SERVES 4

PREPARATION TIME 10 MINUTES

COOKING TIME 20 MINUTES

INGREDIENTS

175 g / 6 oz / 1 cup quinoa, rinsed in cold
    water and drained
55 ml / 2 fl. oz / ¼ cup extra-virgin olive oil
1 lemon, juiced
400 g / 14 oz / 2 cups canned chickpeas
    (garbanzo beans), drained
150 g / 5 oz / 1 cup cherry tomatoes, halved
1 small cucumber, seeded and diced
a small bunch of flat-leaf parsley,
    roughly chopped
salt and freshly ground black pepper

METHOD

- Place the quinoa in a large, heavy-based
  saucepan. Cook over a low heat, stirring
  continuously until the grains separate.

- Stir in 550 ml / 1 pt 1 fl. oz / 2 ⅓ cups
  of water and a little salt, then cook
  until boiling.

- Reduce to a simmer and cook for
  15 minutes or until the liquid has been
  absorbed. Transfer to a mixing bowl and
  leave to cool.

- Whisk together the olive oil and lemon
  juice in a mixing bowl and dress the
  quinoa with it.

- Add the chickpeas, cherry tomatoes,
  cucumber and parsley. Fold gently but
  thoroughly into the quinoa and season
  to taste.

- Spoon into bowls before serving.

TOP TIP
This salad can be served
warm or cold.

Meat and Fish Dishes

Chicken and Apricot Tagine

SERVES 4

PREPARATION TIME 15 MINUTES

COOKING TIME 1 HOUR

INGREDIENTS

75 ml / 3 fl. oz / ⅓ cup olive oil
4 chicken legs, trimmed
4 chicken drumsticks, trimmed
1 onion, finely chopped
2 cloves of garlic, minced
2 x 5 cm (2 in) sticks of cinnamon
1 tsp mild curry powder
1 tsp ras el hanout
1 tsp ground cumin
225 g / 8 oz / 1 ½ cups dried apricot halves
1 tbsp honey
750 ml / 1 pint 6 fl. oz / 3 cups chicken stock
2 tbsp pine nuts
a small bunch of coriander (cilantro),
    roughly chopped
salt and freshly ground black pepper

METHOD

- Heat half of the olive oil in a large casserole dish or tagine set over a moderate heat until hot.

- Season the chicken pieces with plenty of salt and pepper. Seal in the oil, in batches, until golden all over.

- Remove from the dish and add the onion, garlic and cinnamon stick. Fry for 4–5 minutes, stirring frequently, until lightly browned.

- Add the ground spices, stir well, and continue to cook over a reduced heat for 1 minute.

- Return the chicken to the dish along with the apricots, honey and stock. Stir well and cook until simmering.

- Cover with a lid and cook over a low heat for 40–45 minutes until the chicken is cooked through.

- Season to taste with salt and pepper. Serve in a large bowl, garnished with pine nuts and coriander.

TOP TIP

Replace the apricots with dried prunes for a different fruity take on this tagine.

Chicken Breast with Pancetta

RVES 4

EPARATION TIME 10 MINUTES

OKING TIME 50 MINUTES

GREDIENTS

- kinless chicken breasts, trimmed
- 0 g / 5 oz / 1 ½ cups sliced mozzarella
- lices of pancetta
- osp olive oil
- 0 ml / 1 pint 2 fl. oz / 2 ½ cups chicken stock
- ml / 2 fl. oz / ¼ cup single cream
- 0 g / 10 ½ oz / 2 cups heirloom cherry tomatoes
- mall handful of sage leaves
- t and freshly ground black pepper

METHOD

- Preheat the oven to 190°C (170°C fan) / 375F / gas 5.
- Butterfly the chicken breasts with a sharp knife, then stuff with the mozzarella and season with salt and pepper.
- Wrap well with the pancetta and drizzle with olive oil. Season again with salt and pepper and place in a roasting tray.
- Pour the stock around the chicken and roast for 40–45 minutes until the breasts are cooked through.
- Remove from the oven and stir through the cream. Garnish with cherry tomatoes and sage leaves before serving.

TOP TIP
Baste the chicken occasionally with the stock in the dish when roasting.

Chicken and Pineapple Pizza

MAKES 2

PREPARATION TIME 15 MINUTES

COOKING TIME 10 MINUTES

INGREDIENTS

2 x 20 cm (8 in) gluten-free pizza bases
225 g / 8 oz / 1 cup barbecue sauce
125 g / 4 ½ oz / 1 ¼ cups grated mozzarella
150 g / 5 oz / 1 cup cherry tomatoes, halved
1 green pepper, thinly sliced
2 large, cooked, skinless chicken
    breasts, sliced
200 g / 7 oz / 1 cup canned pineapple
    chunks, drained
2 tbsp olive oil
a small handful of red chard
100 g / 3 ½ oz / 2 cups watercress
55 g / 2 oz / 1 cup lettuce leaves
salt and freshly ground black pepper

METHOD

- Preheat the oven to 230°C (210°C fan) / 450F / gas 8 and place two large, round baking trays in the oven to preheat.

- Spread the pizza bases with barbecue sauce. Top with mozzarella, cherry tomatoes, pepper, chicken, and pineapple chunks.

- Drizzle with olive oil and season with salt and pepper, then bake for 8–10 minutes until the bases are cooked through and the cheese has melted.

- Remove from the oven and serve immediately with a garnish of chard, watercress, and lettuce leaves.

TOP TIP
Substitute the chicken for canned artichoke hearts for vegetarian pizzas.

Glazed Duck

RVES 4

EPARATION TIME 15 MINUTES

OKING TIME 25 MINUTES

GREDIENTS

osp limoncello
osp honey
arge duck breasts, skin scored
osp olive oil
0 g / 12 oz / 3 cups cooked wild rice
t and freshly ground black pepper

METHOD

- Preheat the oven to 190°C (170°C fan) / 375F / gas 5. Stir together the limoncello and honey in a small bowl.

- Season the duck breasts and place skin-side down in a cast-iron frying pan. Set the pan over a medium heat and cook until most of the fat has rendered away.

- Pour away all but 1 tbsp of the fat and flip the breasts. Brush the skin with the limoncello and honey using a pastry brush.

- Move the duck breasts to the oven. Roast for 6–10 minutes depending on desired degree of cooking.

- Remove the duck from the oven and move to a plate. Cover loosely with aluminium foil and leave to rest for 10 minutes.

- Heat the oil in a large saucepan set over a moderate heat until hot. Add the rice, season with salt and pepper, and fry in the oil until piping hot.

- Slice the duck and serve with bowls of rice.

TOP TIP

When scoring the duck breasts, make sure that you score the skin and fat only.

Turkey Enchiladas

SERVES 4

PREPARATION TIME 35 MINUTES

COOKING TIME 45 MINUTES

INGREDIENTS

2 tbsp olive oil

1 medium onion, chopped

1 clove of garlic, finely chopped

2 small turkey breasts, chopped

2 tbsp tomato purée

250 ml / 9 fl. oz / 1 cup chicken stock, approx.

200 g / 7 oz / 1 cup canned sweetcorn,
  drained

200 g / 7 oz / 1 cup canned kidney beans,
  drained

a pinch of Cayenne

8 gluten-free tortillas

400 g / 14 oz / 2 cups canned chopped
  tomatoes

100 g / 3 ½ oz / 1 cup Cheddar, grated

a small handful of coriander (cilantro),
  chopped

salt and freshly ground black pepper

METHOD

- Preheat the oven to 200°C (180°C fan) / 400F / gas 6.
- Heat the olive oil in a pan and fry the onion and garlic briefly. Add the turkey and continue to fry until golden brown.
- Mix in the tomato purée and add the stock. Add the sweetcorn and kidney beans, season with salt and pepper and simmer for roughly 15 minutes until slightly thickened.
- Remove from the heat and season to taste with the Cayenne and more salt and pepper.
- Spread the filling onto the tortillas and roll them up. Lay them side-by-side in an ovenproof dish.
- Top with the tomatoes and cheese. Cook in the oven for 20–25 minutes until golden brown.
- Remove from the oven and garnish with coriander leaves before serving.

TOP TIP

Remove the Cayenne for a less spicy take on these enchiladas.

Massaman Beef Curry

SERVES 4

PREPARATION TIME 15 MINUTES

COOKING TIME 15 MINUTES

INGREDIENTS

2 tbsp groundnut oil

2 tbsp Massaman curry paste

1 tsp dried red chilli (chili) flakes

600 g / 1 lb 5 oz / 4 cups rump steak, cut into thin strips

1 large onion, finely sliced

400 g / 12 oz / 3 cups green (string) beans, trimmed

150 g / 5 oz / 1 ½ cups baby sweetcorn

250 ml / 9 fl. oz / 1 cup beef stock

225 ml / 8 fl. oz / 1 cup coconut milk

1 lime, juiced

1 tbsp chilli (chili) sauce

coriander (cilantro) sprigs, to garnish

Salt and freshly ground black pepper

METHOD

- Heat the oil in a large wok or shallow pan set over a moderate heat until hot.

- Stir the curry paste and chilli flakes into the oil, cooking for 1 minute.

- Add the rump steak and fry for 3–4 minutes, stirring occasionally. Add the vegetables, stir well, then cook for a further 2 minutes.

- Cover with the stock and coconut milk. Cook until simmering, then reduce the heat and cook the curry steadily for 5 minutes.

- Season to taste with lime juice, chilli sauce, salt and pepper. Garnish with coriander sprigs.

TOP TIP

Use light coconut milk for a lighter version of this curry.

Beef and Carrot Pie

MAKES 2

PREPARATION TIME 20 MINUTES

COOKING TIME 1 HOUR 45 MINUTES

INGREDIENTS

2 tbsp sunflower oil

750 g / 1 lb 10 oz / 5 cups chuck steak, trimmed and cubed

4 large carrots, peeled, halved, and sliced

500 ml / 18 fl. oz / 2 cups beef stock

2 tbsp cornflour (cornstarch)

225 g / 8 oz ready-made gluten-free puff pastry

a little gluten-free plain (all-purpose) flour, for dusting

1 large egg, beaten

1 tbsp whole milk

2 tbsp unsalted butter

250 g / 9 oz / 2 cups green (string) beans, trimmed

6 spring onions (scallions), trimmed

salt and freshly ground black pepper

METHOD

- Preheat the oven to 180°C (160°C fan) / 350F / gas 4. Heat the oil in a casserole d set over a moderate heat until hot. Seaso the beef and seal in batches until golden.

- Reduce the heat a little and add the carro Cook for 4–5 minutes, stirring occasiona then cover with the stock. Cook until simmering, then reduce to a low heat. Cover and cook gently for 55–60 minute until the beef and carrots are tender.

- Whisk the cornflour with 2 tbsp of wate make a paste. Whisk the paste into the be gravy to thicken. Season to taste with sa and pepper, then set to one side.

- Roll out the pastry on a lightly floured surface to 1 cm (½ in) thickness. Cut into two rectangles approximately 15 cm (6 i x 8 cm (3 in) in dimension.

- Fill two individual baking dishes with the beef, carrots and gravy. Drape over the pastry, sealing well against the edges Trim away any excess, overhanging past

- Beat together the egg and milk and brush over the tops of the pastry. Bore a small h in the centres and sit the dishes on a bak tray. Bake for 30–35 minutes until the pastry if puffed and golden.

- Melt the butter in a large frying pan. Add the beans and spring onions, then c for 4–5 minutes until tender. Season to ta and serve with the pies.

TOP TIP

Wet the rims of the dishes with a little water to help the pastry stick.

Mexican Chilli Con Carne

SERVES 4

PREPARATION TIME 15 MINUTES

COOKING TIME 1 HOUR 15 MINUTES

INGREDIENTS

ml / 2 fl. oz / ¼ cup sunflower oil

g / 1 lb 5 oz / 4 cups rump steak, trimmed and cubed

p paprika

sp dried oregano

sp chilli (chili) powder

sp cornflour (cornstarch)

sp gluten-free cocoa powder

g / 7 oz / 1 cup passata

ml / 9 fl. oz / 1 cup beef stock

g / 14 oz / 2 cups canned kidney beans, drained

g / 14 oz / 3 cups cooked long-grain rice

mall avocado, pitted and diced

um tomatoes, cored and diced

t and freshly ground black pepper

METHOD

- Heat the oil in a large casserole dish set over a moderate heat until hot.

- Season the steak and seal, in batches, until brown all over. Reduce the heat a little and add the ground spices, cornflour and cocoa powder.

- Stir well and cook for 1 minute, then cover with the passata, stock and beans.

- Once the chilli starts to simmer, cover the dish with a lid and cook over a slightly reduced heat for 1 hour, until the beef is tender.

- Season to taste with salt and pepper. Serve over bowls of rice, garnished with avocado and tomato.

TOP TIP
Flank or skirt steak would be ideal alternatives to rump in this chilli.

Cheeseburgers

SERVES 4

PREPARATION TIME 15 MINUTES

COOKING TIME 20 MINUTES

INGREDIENTS

600 g / 1 lb 5 oz / 4 cups steak mince
4 rashers of streaky bacon, chopped
150 g / 5 oz / 1 ½ cups Cheddar, sliced
4 gluten-free multigrain rolls, split in half
2 tbsp mayonnaise
55 g / 2 oz / 1 cup rocket (arugula)
75 g / 2 ½ oz / ⅓ cup tomato ketchup
1 large beef tomato, sliced
salt and freshly ground black pepper

METHOD

- Preheat the oven to 220°C (200°C fan) / 425F / gas 8.
- Mix the steak mince with plenty of salt and pepper in a large mixing bowl. Divide the mixture into four and shape into patties.
- Place on a large baking tray and place a thumbprint in the centre of each patty.
- Bake for 15 minutes or until the burgers register at least 70°C / 158F on a meat thermometer. Remove from the oven, top with the bacon and Cheddar, and return to the oven for 4–5 minutes until melted and golden.
- Remove the patties from the oven and leave to rest to one side. Toast the rolls in the oven for 2 minutes.
- Remove the rolls and spread the bottom halves with mayonnaise. Top with rocket leaves and then the patties.
- Top with ketchup, tomato slices and the top of the rolls before serving.

TOP TIP
Check on the rolls after one minute in the oven as they may only need that long.

Steak with Chips

SERVES 4

PREPARATION TIME 15 MINUTES

COOKING TIME 25 MINUTES

INGREDIENTS

5 l / 2 pints 4 fl. oz / 5 cups vegetable oil

200 g / 7 oz sirloin steaks, trimmed

sp groundnut oil

g / 14 oz / 3 cups frozen chips

ml / 3 fl. oz / ⅓ cup extra-virgin olive oil

sp balsamic vinegar

g / 5 oz / 3 cups mixed leaf salad

rge round tomato

and freshly ground black pepper

METHOD

- Heat the oil in a large, heavy-based saucepan until it registers 180°C / 356F on a thermometer. Keep the oil at this temperature as you prepare the steaks.

- Rub the sirloin steaks with groundnut oil and season with salt and pepper. Heat a large cast-iron pan set over a high heat until smoking hot.

- Carefully lay the steaks in the pan. Let the steaks seal, undisturbed, for 4 minutes. Turn the steaks and cook for another 3 minutes.

- Remove the steaks to a plate and leave to rest, covered loosely with kitchen foil, for 10 minutes.

- Deep-fry the chips in the hot oil for 4–5 minutes until golden-brown and crisp. Drain on kitchen paper.

- Whisk together the oil and vinegar and use it to dress the mixed lead salad and tomato. Season with salt and pepper.

- Serve the chips with the steaks and salad on the side.

TOP TIP

Rib-eye or rump would be good alternatives to sirloin.

Piri-piri Pork Belly

SERVES 4

PREPARATION TIME 15 MINUTES

COOKING TIME 1 HOUR 45 MINUTES

INGREDIENTS

75 ml / 3 fl. oz / ⅓ cup olive oil
75 ml / 3 fl. oz / ⅓ cup mild piri-piri sauce
1 clove of garlic, minced
1 kg / 2 lb 4 oz piece of pork belly
    fillet, trimmed
100 g / 3 ½ oz / 2 cups mixed salad leaves
4 gluten-free tortillas
1 red chilli (chili), sliced
5 cm (2 in) lemon grass stalk, finely sliced
salt and freshly ground black pepper

METHOD

- Preheat the oven to 180°C (160°C fan) / 350F / gas 4.
- Whisk together the olive oil, piri-piri sauce, garlic and seasoning in a small mixing bowl. Smear over the pork belly and sit in a roasting dish. Season with more salt and pepper.
- Cover with kitchen foil and roast for 1 hour, then remove the foil and roast for a further 30–35 minutes uncovered, until golden brown on top.
- Remove from the oven and leave to rest covered loosely, for at least 10 minutes.
- Serve the pork with salad leaves and tortillas on the side, garnished with chilli and lemon grass on top.

TOP TIP
Baste the pork belly from time to time when roasting.

Roasted Pork Chops with Sage

SERVES 4

PREPARATION TIME 15 MINUTES

COOKING TIME 25 MINUTES

INGREDIENTS

g / 1 lb 10 oz / 5 cups butternut squash, cubed

one-in pork chops, trimmed

sp sunflower oil

ml / 3 fl. oz / ⅓ cup olive oil

ml / 3 fl. oz / ⅓ cup double (heavy) cream

rge bunch of sage leaves, picked

mon, cut into wedges

and freshly ground black pepper

METHOD

- Preheat the oven to 190°C (170°C fan) / 375F / gas 5.

- Cook the butternut squash in a large saucepan of salted, boiling water for 15–20 minutes until tender to the point of a knife.

- Meanwhile, rub the pork chops with sunflower oil and season with salt and pepper. Place in a roasting tray and roast for 18–20 minutes until they register at least 70°C / 158F on a meat thermometer.

- Drain the squash when ready and leave to steam off for a few minutes, then mash with the olive oil, cream, and seasoning.

- Remove the pork chops from the oven and leave to rest for at least 5 minutes, covered loosely.

- Spoon the butternut squash purée onto plates and serve with the chops, sage leaves, and lemon wedges.

TOP TIP

The pork chops can be left to rest for up to 15 minutes before serving.

One-pot Gammon Stew

SERVES 4

PREPARATION TIME 15 MINUTES

COOKING TIME 40 MINUTES

INGREDIENTS

2 tbsp olive oil

2 large carrots, peeled and diced

1 small turnip, peeled and diced

600 g / 1 lb 5 oz / 4 cups gammon steak,
  trimmed

1 l / 1 pint 16 fl. oz / 4 cups low-sodium
  vegetable stock

55 g / 2 oz / 1 cup watercress, roughly
  chopped

a large handful of flat-leaf parsley, chopped

salt and freshly ground black pepper

METHOD

- Heat the olive oil in a large casserole dish set over a medium heat until hot.

- Add the carrot, turnip and a little salt. Sweat for 5–6 minutes, stirring occasionally, until softened.

- Add the gammon and stock, then stir well. Simmer for 25–30 minutes until the gammon is tender.

- Remove the gammon from the dish and roughly shred between two forks. Stir back into the dish.

- Stir through the watercress and parsley. Season to taste with salt and pepper before serving from the dish.

TOP TIP

Rinse the gammon in cold water to remove any salty residue.

Sausages with Mash and Gravy

SERVES 4

PREPARATION TIME 15 MINUTES

COOKING TIME 40 MINUTES

INGREDIENTS

1 kg / 2 lb 4 oz / 6 ⅔ cups floury potatoes, peeled and diced

2 tbsp sunflower oil

2 small red onions, halved

400 ml / 14 fl oz / 1 ⅔ cups low-sodium beef stock

100 ml / 3 ½ fl oz / ½ cup red wine

1 tbsp cornflour (cornstarch)

50 g / 3 ½ oz / ½ cup butter

8 small gluten-free pork sausages, pricked with a fork

Salt and freshly ground black pepper

METHOD

- Preheat the grill to hot.

- Cook the potato in a large saucepan of salted, boiling water for 18–22 minutes until tender to the point of a knife.

- Heat the oil in a large saucepan set over a moderate heat until hot. Add the onions and fry for 2 minutes, then cover with the stock and red wine.

- Increase the heat until boiling. Reduce the gravy over a moderate heat until slightly thickened. Whisk the cornflour with 2 tbsp of water and whisk a little into the simmering gravy until thickened to your liking.

- Season to taste with salt and pepper, then keep warm to one side.

- Drain the potatoes and leave them to steam off for a few minutes, then mash with the butter and plenty of seasoning until smooth. Keep warm to one side.

- Arrange the sausages on a grilling tray, spaced apart. Grill for 8–10 minutes, turning occasionally, until golden brown all over and cooked through.

- Spoon the mashed potato into bowls and top with the gravy. Serve the sausages alongside.

TOP TIP

Dice the potatoes to the same size for an even cooking time.

Lamb Shoulder

SERVES 4

PREPARATION TIME 15 MINUTES

COOKING TIME 1 HOUR 40 MINUTES

INGREDIENTS

1.25 kg / 2 lb 12 oz piece of lamb shoulder,
    trimmed and scored
100 ml / 3 ½ fl. oz / ½ cup tbsp olive oil
2 tsp mild curry powder
a small bunch of rosemary, chopped
1 tbsp coriander seeds, crushed
300 g / 10 ½ oz / 2 cups new potatoes, halved
salt and freshly ground black pepper

METHOD

- Preheat the oven to 180°C (160°C fan) / 350F / gas 4.
- Rub the lamb shoulder with half of the olive oil. Massage the curry powder, rosemary, crushed coriander seeds and seasoning into the meat.
- Arrange the potatoes in the base of a roasting dish and drizzle with the remaining oil. Sit the lamb on top.
- Cover with aluminium foil and roast for 1 hour.
- Remove the foil and continue to roast for a further 30 minutes uncovered.
- Remove from the oven and leave to rest for 10 minutes, covered loosely, before serving.

TOP TIP

The lamb can be left to rest for up to 30 minutes before serving.

Lamb Chops with Tomato Salsa

SERVES 4

PREPARATION TIME 15 MINUTES

COOKING TIME 25 MINUTES

INGREDIENTS

- bone-in lamb chops, trimmed
- tbsp sunflower oil
- aubergines (eggplants), split in half
- tbsp balsamic vinegar
- ml / 2 fl. oz / ¼ cup olive oil
- tbsp distilled vinegar
- lime, juiced
- tsp caster (superfine) sugar
- g / 1 lb / 3 cups vine tomatoes, cored, seeded and diced
- small red onion, finely chopped
- clove of garlic, minced
- small bunch of coriander (cilantro), roughly chopped
- g / 5 oz / 1 ½ cups asparagus, woody ends removed
- salt and freshly ground black pepper

METHOD

- Preheat the oven to 190°C (170°C fan) / 375F / gas 5.
- Rub the lamb chops with sunflower oil and season with salt and pepper. Position in a roasting tray and brush the aubergine with balsamic vinegar. Season with salt and pepper and position alongside the lamb chops.
- Roast for 18–20 minutes until the lamb registers at least 70°C / 158F on a meat thermometer.
- Meanwhile, stir together the olive oil, vinegar, lime juice, sugar and seasoning in a mixing bowl. Add the tomato, red onion, garlic, chopped coriander and stir well. Cover and set to one side.
- Remove the lamb chops from the oven once ready and leave to rest for at least 5 minutes, covered loosely. Return the aubergine to the oven for a further 5 minutes.
- Cook the asparagus in a large saucepan of salted, boiling water for 3 minutes until tender. Drain well and season with salt and pepper.
- Serve the chops on plates with the salsa, roast aubergine, and asparagus on the side.

TOP TIP

Prepare the salsa a day ahead of serving for better results.

Oven-poached Cod

SERVES 4

PREPARATION TIME 15 MINUTES

COOKING TIME 20 MINUTES

INGREDIENTS

2 large shallots, chopped

450 g / 1 lb / 3 cups vine tomatoes, cored
and diced

2 yellow peppers, chopped

55 ml / 2 fl. oz / ¼ cup extra-virgin olive oil

1 bunch of chives

4 x 175 g / 6 oz cod fillets, pin-boned and
trimmed

250 ml / 9 fl. oz / 1 cup vegetable stock

1 lemon, sliced

salt and freshly ground black pepper

METHOD

- Preheat the oven to 190°C (170°C fan) /
  375F / gas 5.

- Pulse together the shallot, tomato,
  pepper, olive oil and most of the
  chives in a food processor until finely
  chopped. Season to taste with salt and
  pepper and set to one side.

- Place the cod in a roasting dish and
  pour over the stock. Season with salt
  and pepper and cover the dish with
  kitchen foil.

- Bake in the oven for 12–14 minutes
  until the cod is cooked through
  and flaking.

- Remove from the oven and lift onto
  plates using a fish slice. Top with the
  chopped salsa.

- Garnish with slices of lemon and the
  remaining chives before serving.

TOP TIP

A pair of kitchen tweezers are ideal for pin-boning the cod fillets.

Salmon Fillets

SERVES 4

PREPARATION TIME 15 MINUTES

COOKING TIME 15 MINUTES

INGREDIENTS

- large mango, pitted, peeled and diced
- small bunch of coriander (cilantro), chopped
- red onion, finely chopped
- g / 10 ½ oz / 2 cups vine tomatoes, cored, seeded, and diced
- limes
- 175 g / 6 oz salmon fillets
- tbsp olive oil
- and freshly ground black pepper

METHOD

- Preheat the oven to 200°C (180°C fan) / 400F / gas 6.

- Stir together the mango, coriander, onion, and tomatoes in a mixing bowl. Juice and zest one of the limes into the bowl, stirring well. Season to taste with salt and pepper.

- Arrange the salmon fillets on a baking tray lined with greaseproof paper. Drizzle with olive oil and season with salt and pepper.

- Bake for 12–14 minutes until firm yet slightly springy to the touch.

- Remove from the oven and lift onto plates. Top with the mango salad and cut the remaining lime into wedges, serving them alongside the salad.

TOP TIP
Sea bass works equally well in this recipe.

Chargrilled Tuna

SERVES 4

PREPARATION TIME 15 MINUTES

COOKING TIME 15 MINUTES

INGREDIENTS

4 x 200 g / 7 oz tuna steaks
2 tbsp sunflower oil
55 g / 2 oz / ½ cup sunflower seeds
350 g / 12 oz / 3 cups green (string) beans
2 tbsp olive oil
1 red chilli (chili), chopped
1 lime, cut into wedges
salt and freshly ground black pepper

METHOD

- Rub the tuna steaks with sunflower oil and press the edges into sesame seeds. Season with salt and pepper.

- Heat a large griddle pan over a moderate heat until hot and seal the tuna steaks in the pan for 3 minutes. Flip, then cook for another 2 minutes until firm yet springy to the touch.

- Remove the tuna steaks to a plate and cover loosely with kitchen foil.

- Cook the green beans in a large saucepan of salted, boiling water for 2 minutes. Drain well and leave to cool slightly.

- Heat the olive oil in a large frying pan set over a moderate heat until hot. Add the chilli, fry for 1 minute, then add the beans.

- Cook for a further minute and season to taste with salt and pepper.

- Serve the tuna steaks over the beans, garnished with lime wedges on the side.

TOP TIP

A small handful of flaked (slivered) almonds adds a welcome crunch to this dish.

Garlic Mussels

SERVES 4

PREPARATION TIME 10 MINUTES

COOKING TIME 10 MINUTES

INGREDIENTS

2 bsp olive oil

2 loves of garlic, crushed

600 g / 1 lb 5 oz / 4 cups mussels, rinsed with beards removed

175 ml / 6 fl. oz / ¾ cup dry white wine

1 large bunch of coriander (cilantro)

2 red chillies (chilies), seeded and sliced

Salt and freshly ground black pepper

METHOD

- Heat the oil in a large saucepan set over a moderate heat until hot.

- Add the garlic and fry for 30 seconds, then add the mussels. Increase the heat, add the wine, then cover the pan with a lid.

- Cook over a slightly reduced heat for 4–5 minutes, shaking the pan occasionally, until the mussels have opened. Discard any that don't open.

- Chop half of the coriander and stir into the mussels along with the chilli. Season to taste with salt and pepper.

- Ladle into bowls and serve with a garnish of the remaining coriander.

TOP TIP

Discard any mussels that don't close with a tap before cooking them.

Vegetable Dishes

Stuffed Red Peppers

SERVES 4

PREPARATION TIME 15 MINUTES

COOKING TIME 35 MINUTES

INGREDIENTS

225 g / 8 oz / 2 cups feta, cubed
225 g / 8 oz / 2 cups mozzarella, drained and diced
55 ml / 2 fl. oz / ¼ cup olive oil
a small bunch of flat-leaf parsley, chopped
4 large red peppers, halved
salt and freshly ground black pepper

METHOD

- Preheat the oven to 190°C (170°C fan) / 375F / gas 5.
- Toss together the cheeses in a mixing bowl with 2 tbsp of oil, the parsley and some seasoning.
- Spoon into the pepper halves and arrange them in a roasting tray.
- Drizzle with the remaining oil. Roast for 25–30 minutes until the peppers are tender.
- Remove from the oven and leave to stand briefly before serving.

TOP TIP
Try a mixture of yellow, green and red peppers.

Stuffed Baked Mushrooms

SERVES 4

PREPARATION TIME 15 MINUTES

COOKING TIME 55 MINUTES

INGREDIENTS

600 g / 1 lb 5 oz / 4 cups floury potatoes, peeled and diced

50 g / 2 oz / ¼ cup unsalted butter

small handful of oregano, chopped

1 shallot, finely chopped

2 cloves of garlic, minced

4 portobello mushrooms, peeled

60 ml / 2 fl. oz / ¼ cup olive oil

2 large vine tomatoes, cored, seeded, and diced

small bunch of chervil

salt and freshly ground black pepper

METHOD

- Cook the potatoes in a large saucepan of salted, boiling water for 15–20 minutes until soft to the point of a knife.

- Preheat the oven to 190°C (170°C fan) / 375F / gas 5.

- Drain the potatoes and leave to steam off for a few minutes, then mash with the butter, oregano, shallot, garlic and seasoning.

- Remove the stalks from the mushrooms and finely chop, then mash into the potato.

- Fill the mushroom caps with the potato mixture and arrange in a baking dish. Drizzle with olive oil and season with salt and pepper.

- Bake for 25–30 minutes until the mushrooms are tender to the point of a knife.

- Remove from the oven and top with the tomatoes and a garnish of chervil before serving.

TOP TIP

Add a handful of pancetta lardons to the stuffing.

Mushroom Tart

SERVES 4

PREPARATION TIME 15 MINUTES

COOKING TIME 1 HOUR 20 MINUTES

INGREDIENTS

250 g / 9 oz ready-made gluten-free
    shortcrust pastry
a little gluten-free plain (all-purpose) flour,
    for dusting
2 tbsp olive oil
1 clove of garlic, minced
450 g / 1 lb / 6 cups mixed wild mushrooms,
    brushed clean
8 large eggs
250 ml / 9 fl. oz / 1 cup whole milk
150 g / 5 oz / 1 ½ cups goats' cheese, crumbled
a small handful of flat-leaf parsley
100 g / 3 ½ oz / 2 cups rocket (arugula)
salt and freshly ground black pepper

METHOD

- Preheat the oven to 170°C (150°C fan) /
  325F / gas 3.

- Roll out the pastry on a lightly floured
  surface to 1 cm (½ in) thickness. Use it to
  line a 20 cm (7 in) pie dish, then cut away
  any excess and prick the base with a fork.

- Heat the olive oil in a large frying pan set
  over a moderate heat until hot. Add the
  garlic and fry for 30 seconds, then add the
  mushrooms and a little seasoning.

- Fry for 5 minutes, tossing occasionally,
  until softened, then season to taste.

- Spoon most of the mushrooms into the
  pastry case. Beat together the eggs,
  milk, goats' cheese and seasoning in
  a mixing bowl.

- Pour over the mushrooms and transfer to
  the oven. Bake for 1 hour 5–10 minutes
  until the pastry is cooked through and the
  filling is set and golden on top.

- Remove from the oven and leave to stand
  for 5 minutes. Turn out from the dish and
  cut into portions.

- Serve with the remaining mushrooms, a
  garnish of parsley and some rocket leaves
  on the side.

TOP TIP

Soak the mushrooms briefly in cold water to remove any dirt before cooking.

Vegetable Curry

SERVES 4

PREPARATION TIME 15 MINUTES

COOKING TIME 40 MINUTES

INGREDIENTS

ml / 2 fl. oz / ¼ cup sunflower oil

large onion, sliced

yellow pepper, sliced

cloves of garlic, minced

cm (2 in) root ginger, peeled and minced

small red chilli (chili), seeded and finely
chopped

tsp ground cumin

tsp ground coriander

tsp garam masala

small head of broccoli, prepared into
small florets

0 g / 5 oz / 2 cups button mushrooms,
brushed clean and chopped

0 g / 10 ½ oz / 2 cups okra, split in half

0 ml / 18 fl. oz / 2 cups vegetable stock

small bunch of coriander (cilantro),
roughly chopped

g / 2 oz / ½ cup hazelnuts (cobnuts),
lightly crushed

g / 2 oz / ½ cup flaked (slivered) almonds

t and freshly ground black pepper

METHOD

- Heat the oil in a large casserole dish
  set over a medium heat until hot.
- Add the onion, pepper, garlic, ginger,
  chilli and a little salt, then fry for
  8–10 minutes until golden, stirring
  occasionally.
- Add the ground spices, stir well and
  cook for a further minute. Stir in the
  broccoli, mushrooms and okra.
- Cook for a further 2 minutes and
  stir in the stock. Once simmering,
  cook over a slightly reduced heat for
  15–20 minutes until all the vegetables
  are tender.
- Season to taste with salt and pepper.
  Garnish with coriander and nuts
  before serving.

TOP TIP

Add more or less of the
spices to suit your
tastes.

Pumpkin Quiches

MAKES 4

PREPARATION TIME 20 MINUTES

COOKING TIME 40 MINUTES

INGREDIENTS

200 g / 7 oz ready-made gluten-free filo
    pastry, kept under a damp cloth
55 g / 2 oz / ¼ cup unsalted butter, melted
250 ml / 9 fl. oz / 1 cup crème fraiche
250 ml / 9 fl. oz / 1 cup whole milk
200 g / 7 oz / 1 cup pumpkin purée
4 large eggs
100 g / 3 ½ oz / 1 cup goats' cheese, crumbled
2 plum tomatoes, seeded and diced
2 sprigs of thyme, finely chopped
salt and freshly ground black pepper

METHOD

- Preheat the oven to 180°C (160°C fan) / 350F / gas 4.

- Line four individual tart tins with sheets of the filo pastry, overlapping and fitting them to size. Brush the pastry with melted butter.

- Whisk together the crème fraiche, milk, pumpkin purée, eggs and seasoning until smooth, then fold through the goats' cheese.

- Pour into the cases and top with diced tomato and chopped thyme. Transfer the cases to a baking tray.

- Bake the quiches for 35–40 minutes until golden at the edges and the tops are set.

- Remove to a wire rack to cool before serving.

TOP TIP

These quiches can be served warm or cold.

Vegetable Moussaka

SERVES 4

PREPARATION TIME 20 MINUTES

COOKING TIME 1 HOUR 30 MINUTES

INGREDIENTS

aubergines (eggplants), sliced
ml / 2 fl. oz / ¼ cup olive oil
small onions, finely chopped
cloves of garlic, minced
g / 1 lb / 3 cups vine tomatoes, sliced
dried oregano
dried thyme
tsp ground cinnamon
/ 2 ½ oz / ⅓ cup unsalted butter
/ 2 oz / ⅓ cup gluten-free plain
(all-purpose) flour
cornflour (cornstarch)
ml / 1 pint 6 fl. oz / 3 cups whole milk
small egg yolks
g / 4 oz / 1 cup Cheddar, grated
g / 12 oz / 1 ½ cups ricotta
small handful of coriander (cilantro)
and freshly ground black pepper

METHOD

- Salt the aubergine slices and arrange on kitchen paper to drain for 10 minutes. Pat dry and set to one side.

- Heat the oil in a casserole dish set over a medium heat, then sauté the onion and garlic for 4–5 minutes. Add the sliced tomatoes and cook for a further 2 minutes, then stir in the dried herbs and spices.

- Add 200 ml / 7 fl. oz / ¾ cup of water and simmer. Cook for 15 minutes over a reduced heat until thickened, then season.

- Preheat the oven to 190°C (170°C fan) / 375F / gas 5. Melt the butter in a large saucepan set over a moderate heat. Whisk in the flour and cornflour to make a roux, cooking it until golden.

- Whisk in the milk in a slow, steady stream until thickened and simmer for 5 minutes. Whisk in the egg yolks, cheese and some seasoning.

- Spoon a little of the tomato sauce into the base of a large baking dish and top with aubergine slices, ricotta and some cheese sauce. Repeat twice and finish with slices of aubergine and cheese sauce on top.

- Bake for 40–45 minutes until golden-brown on top. Remove from the oven and leave to stand briefly before serving with a garnish of coriander.

TOP TIP
Grease the baking dish with a little oil before layering the moussaka.

Vegetable Fajitas

METHOD

- Heat the oil in a large frying pan set over a moderate heat until hot.
- Add all of the vegetables, along with the chilli and a pinch of salt. Fry for 7–8 minutes, tossing occasionally until golden.
- Sprinkle over the ground spices and add 2 tbsp of warm water. Continue to cook for 3–4 minutes, stirring occasionally.
- Stir through the chopped coriander and tomatoes. Season to taste with salt and pepper.
- Warm the tortillas in a dry frying pan set over a low heat. Fill with the vegetables and fold.
- Garnish with a drizzle of sour cream and a pinch of smoked paprika before serving.

SERVES 4

PREPARATION TIME 20 MINUTES

COOKING TIME 20 MINUTES

INGREDIENTS

55 ml / 2 fl. oz / ¼ cup sunflower oil
2 onions, sliced
2 green peppers, sliced
2 red peppers, sliced
4 Portobello mushrooms, peeled and sliced
1 red chilli (chili), seeded and sliced
2 tsp paprika
1 tsp ground cumin
1 tsp ground coriander
1 large handful of coriander (cilantro), chopped
2 vine tomatoes, cored, seeded and diced
4 large gluten-free tortillas
110 g / 4 oz / ½ cup sour cream
½ tsp smoked paprika
salt and freshly ground black pepper

TOP TIP
Sprinkle the tortillas with a little water before warming in the pan.

Chickpea Burgers

RVES 4

EPARATION TIME 10 MINUTES

OKING TIME 15 MINUTES

INGREDIENTS

- g / 1 lb 5 oz / 3 cups canned chickpeas (garbanzo beans), drained
- hallot, finely chopped
- g / 2 oz / ⅓ cup cornflour (cornstarch)
- g / 3 ½ oz / ½ cup hummus
- mon, juiced
- ml / 2 fl. oz / ¼ cup olive oil, plus extra for oiling
- um tomatoes, cored and chopped
- ed onion, finely chopped
- mall bunch of flat-leaf parsley, roughly chopped
- and freshly ground black pepper

METHOD

- Pulse the chickpeas in a food processor until roughly chopped, then add the shallot, cornflour, hummus, lemon juice and seasoning.

- Pulse until the mixture comes together yet retains some texture. Shape into patties between oiled palms.

- Heat the olive oil in a large frying pan set over a medium heat until hot. Shallow-fry the patties for 3–4 minutes on both sides, turning once, until golden brown all over.

- Stir together the tomato, red onion, half of the parsley and some seasoning.

- Drain the chickpea burgers on kitchen paper. Serve with the tomato salad and a sprinkling of chopped parsley.

TOP TIP

Tightly pack the mixture when shaping the patties to prevent them from breaking down.

Stuffed Squash

MAKES 4

PREPARATION TIME 15 MINUTES

COOKING TIME 1 HOUR

INGREDIENTS

2 medium butternut squash, split in half with
seeds scooped out
75 ml / 3 fl. oz / ⅓ cup olive oil
2 onions, finely sliced
400 g / 14 oz / 3 cups cooked puy lentils
150 g / 5 oz / 1 ½ cups feta, cubed
a small handful of flat-leaf parsley,
finely chopped
2 tbsp balsamic vinegar
1 pomegranate, halved with seeds removed
55 g / 2 oz / ½ cup pine nuts
salt and freshly ground black pepper

METHOD

- Preheat the oven to 190°C (170°C fan) /
  375F / gas 5.
- Cut out the flesh from two of the
  squash halves and roughly chop, then
  set to one side.
- Heat half of the olive oil in a large
  frying pan set over a medium heat
  until hot. Add the onion and fry for
  3–4 minutes.
- Add the lentils, feta, parsley, chopped
  squash and balsamic vinegar.
- Stir well and cook for a further minute.
  Season to taste with salt and pepper.
- Spoon into the butternut squash
  halves. Arrange in a roasting tray and
  drizzle with the remaining oil.
- Roast for 45–50 minutes until the
  squash is tender to the point of a knife.
- Remove from the oven and garnish
  with pomegranate seeds and pine nuts
  before serving.

TOP TIP
Chervil or chives work
as well as parsley in
this recipe.

Nut Roast

METHOD

- Preheat the oven to 180°C (160°C fan) / 350F / gas 4. Grease and line a 900 g / 2 lb loaf tin with greaseproof paper.
- Combine the peppers, nuts, onions, celery, garlic and seasoning in a food processor. Pulse until finely chopped.
- Scrape into a bowl and add the oil, eggs, cornflour, plain flour, baking powder, Xanthan gum and seasoning.
- Beat well until a batter forms. Scrape the mixture into the prepared loaf tin. Tap the tin a few times to settle the batter.
- Bake for 45–50 minutes until golden on top and risen. A cake tester should come out clean from its centre.
- Remove to a wire rack to cool before turning out, slicing and serving.

SERVES 8

PREPARATION TIME 15 MINUTES

COOKING TIME 1 HOUR

INGREDIENTS

red peppers, chopped
225 g / 8 oz / 2 cups cashews
225 g / 8 oz / 2 cups hazelnuts (cobnuts)
250 g / 9 oz / 2 cups cooked chestnuts, chopped
small onions, finely chopped
stalks of celery, finely chopped
cloves of garlic, minced
75 ml / 3 fl. oz / ⅓ cup sunflower oil
large eggs, beaten
75 g / 2 oz / ⅓ cup cornflour (cornstarch), sifted
100 g / 3 ½ oz / ⅔ cup gluten-free plain (all-purpose) flour, sifted
½ tsp gluten-free baking powder
½ tsp Xanthan gum
salt and freshly ground black pepper

TOP TIP

Fold through a handful of feta or mozzarella for a cheesy addition.

Tomato and Mozzarella Pizza

MAKES 1

PREPARATION TIME 10 MINUTES

COOKING TIME 15 MINUTES

INGREDIENTS

1 large, rectangular, gluten-free pizza crust
200 g / 7 oz / 1 cup passata
1 tsp dried oregano
225 g / 8 oz / 2 cups grated mozzarella
150 g / 5 oz / 1 cup cherry tomatoes, halved
2 tbsp olive oil
a small handful of basil leaves
salt and freshly ground black pepper

METHOD

- Preheat the oven to 230°C (210°C fan) / 450F / gas 8.

- Top the pizza crust with passata, spreading it out evenly to the borders. Sprinkle over half of the oregano and then top with the mozzarella.

- Top with cherry tomato halves and more dried oregano. Drizzle over the olive oil and season with salt and pepper.

- Lift the pizza onto a large, rectangular baking tray. Bake for 10–12 minutes until the crust is cooked through and the cheese is melted and bubbling.

- Remove from the oven and garnish with basil leaves before slicing and serving.

TOP TIP

Preheat the baking tray for 10 minutes in the oven before lifting the dough onto it.

Perfect Roast Potatoes

SERVES 4

PREPARATION TIME 15 MINUTES

COOKING TIME 55 MINUTES

INGREDIENTS

150 g / 5 oz / ⅔ cup duck or goose fat, melted

900 g / 2 lb / 6 cups floury potatoes, peeled and halved

flaked sea salt and freshly ground black pepper

METHOD

- Preheat the oven to 220°C (200°C fan) / 425F / gas 7. Pour the duck or goose fat in a roasting tray and place in the oven to heat up.

- Put the potatoes in a large pan of salted water and cook over a moderate heat until boiling. Boil for 5 minutes then drain well, and return the potatoes to the pan.

- Cover with a lid and shake hard to roughen the surface of the potatoes.

- Remove the hot fat from the oven and carefully add the potatoes, seasoning with salt and pepper.

- Roast for 40–45 minutes, turning once, until the potatoes are golden brown.

TOP TIP

If not available, use sunflower oil instead of the duck or goose fat.

Cakes and Breads

White Chocolate and Raspberry Cake

SERVES 8

PREPARATION TIME 20 MINUTES

COOKING TIME 50 MINUTES

INGREDIENTS

175 g / 6 oz / 1 ¾ cups ground almonds

175 g / 6 oz / ¾ cup unsalted butter, softened

175 g / 6 oz / ¾ cup caster (superfine) sugar

175 g / 6 oz / 1 ¼ cups gluten-free
self-raising flour

1 tsp Xanthan gum

2 large eggs

1 tsp vanilla extract

250 g / 9 oz / 1 ⅔ cups raspberries

150 g / 5 oz / 1 cup white chocolate, melted

2 tbsp freeze-dried raspberries, chopped

METHOD

- Preheat the oven to 180°C (160°C fan) / 350F / gas 4.

- Grease and line a 900 g / 2lb loaf tin with greaseproof paper.

- Place all the ingredients except the raspberries, white chocolate and freeze-dried raspberries in a mixing bowl and beat well until blended.

- Spoon half the batter into the tin and sprinkle over most of the fresh raspberries. Cover with the remaining batter and smooth the top.

- Bake for 45–50 minutes until a skewer inserted into the centre comes out clean. If the cake is browning too quickly, loosely cover the top with foil. Remove to a wire rack to cool.

- Once cool, turn out the cake and spread the melted chocolate over it. Arrange the remaining raspberries on top in a line down the centre.

- Sprinkle over the chopped, freeze-dried raspberries before slicing and serving.

TOP TIP

Tap the tin a few times to help settle the batter before baking.

Carrot Cake

RVES 8

EPARATION TIME 10 MINUTES

OKING TIME 40 MINUTES

GREDIENTS

g / 5 oz / ⅔ cup margarine, softened

g / 5 oz / ⅔ cup caster (superfine) sugar

g / 4 oz / ⅔ cup gluten-free self-raising flour, sifted

sp cornflour (cornstarch)

rge eggs

inch of ground cloves

inch of salt

mall carrots, peeled and finely grated

sp vanilla extract

5 g / 8 oz / 2 cups walnuts

0 g / 10 ½ oz / 1 ½ cups cream cheese

g / 4 oz / ½ cup unsalted butter, softened

5 g / 4 ½ oz / 1 cup icing (confectioners') sugar, sifted

METHOD

- Preheat the oven to 180°C (160°C fan) / 350F / gas 4. Grease and line two 18 cm (7 in) cake tins with greaseproof paper.

- Combine the margarine, sugar, flour, cornflour, eggs, cloves and salt in a large mixing bowl. Beat thoroughly for 2–3 minutes until smooth.

- Add the carrots, vanilla and half of the walnuts. Fold into the batter until incorporated.

- Divide the batter between the two prepared tins, spreading the tops smooth.

- Bake for 20–25 minutes until risen. A cake tester should come out clean from their centres.

- Remove to a wire rack to cool.

- Beat together the cream cheese, butter and icing sugar until smooth. Turn out the sponges and spread the top of one with a third of the icing.

- Sandwich the other sponge on top and spread with the remaining icing. Garnish with the remaining walnuts before slicing and serving.

TOP TIP
To soften the cream cheese, remove it from the fridge before starting.

Banana Cake

SERVES 8

PREPARATION TIME 15 MINUTES

COOKING TIME 1 HOUR 15 MINUTES

INGREDIENTS

250 g / 9 oz / 1 cup butter, softened

350 g / 12 oz / 2 ⅓ cups gluten-free plain (all-purpose) flour

2 ½ tsp gluten-free baking powder

½ tsp bicarbonate of (baking) soda

¼ tsp salt

3 very ripe bananas, mashed

75 ml / 3 fl. oz / ⅓ cup double (heavy) cream

350 g / 12 oz / 1 ½ cups caster (superfine) sugar

4 medium eggs

1 tsp vanilla extract

300 g / 10 ½ oz / 2 cups chocolate chips

METHOD

- Preheat the oven to 160°C (140°C fan) / 325°F / gas 3. Grease a large bundt or ring tin with a little of the butter.

- Put all the ingredients except the chocolate chips into a large mixing bowl and beat with an electric whisk until well-blended, 2–3 minutes. Stir in the chocolate chips.

- Put into the tin and bake for 1 hour 5–15 minutes, until firm and starting to pull away from the sides of the tin.

- Cool in the tin for 15 minutes, and then place on a wire rack to cool completely.

- Turn out, cut into slices, and serve.

TOP TIP

Try a combination of different kinds of chocolate chip.

Fruity Tea Loaf

SERVES 8

PREPARATION TIME 1 HOUR 10 MINUTES

COOKING TIME 1 HOUR 20 MINUTES

INGREDIENTS

- 250 g / 9 oz / 1 ⅔ cups mixed dried fruit
- 250 ml / 9 fl. oz / 1 cup brewed tea
- 1 orange, juiced
- 50 g / 2 oz / ¼ cup unsalted butter, softened
- 100 g / 4 oz / ⅔ cup soft light brown sugar
- 1 large egg, beaten
- 225 g / 8 oz / 1 ½ cups gluten-free plain
  (all-purpose) flour, sifted
- 1 tsp gluten-free baking powder
- pinch of salt
- 200 g / 7 oz / 1 cup ricotta

METHOD

- Preheat the oven to 180°C (160°C fan) / 350F / gas 4.
- Grease and line a 900 g / 2 lb loaf tin with greaseproof paper.
- Mix together the dried fruit, tea and orange juice in a large mixing bowl. Cover and leave to soak for 1 hour.
- Cream together the butter and sugar in a large mixing bowl until smooth and creamy; around 2–3 minutes.
- Beat in the egg, then incorporate the flour in two additions. Fold through the baking powder and salt.
- Fold through the tea-soaked fruit and spoon the batter into the prepared tin, spreading it flat with the back of a wetted tablespoon.
- Bake for 1 hour 5–10 minutes until risen and set. A cake tester should come out clean from its centre when inserted.
- Remove to a wire rack to cool before turning out, slicing, and serving with the ricotta.

TOP TIP
Earl Grey or Assam are ideal teas for this recipe.

Lemon Polenta Cake

SERVES 8

PREPARATION TIME 15 MINUTES

COOKING TIME 50 MINUTES

INGREDIENTS

175 g / 6 oz / ¾ cup unsalted butter, softened

175 g / 6 oz / ¾ cup caster (superfine) sugar

100 g / 3 ½ oz / 1 cup ground almonds

200 g / 7 oz / 1 cup fine polenta

2 tsp gluten-free baking powder

3 medium eggs

½ tsp vanilla extract

2 lemons, zested and juiced

125 g / 4 ½ oz / 1 cup icing (confectioners') sugar

225 g / 8 oz / 1 cup thick cream

METHOD

- Preheat the oven to 190°C (170°C fan) / 3█ / gas 5. Grease and line a 20 cm (8 in) cak█ tin with greaseproof paper.

- Cream together the butter and sugar in a large mixing bowl until pale and fluffy, using an electric hand-held whisk.

- Combine the flour, almonds, polenta and baking powder in a separate mixing bow█ and add one third to the creamed mixtur█ beating well.

- Add 1 egg, beat well, then half the remain█ dry ingredients, followed by another egg. beating well between additions. Repeat a█ with the remaining dry ingredients and e█

- Fold through the vanilla extract and lem█ zest, scraping the batter into the prepare█ cake tin. Bake for 35–40 minutes until gol█ on top and risen. The cake is ready when t█ edges start to shrink away from the sides a█ a cake tester comes out almost clean from █ centre. Remove to a wire rack to cool.

- As the cake cools, whisk together the icin█ sugar and lemon juice in a saucepan unti█ smooth. Cook over a medium heat, stirri█ until the mixture becomes clear and syru█

- Prick the top of the cake all over with a th█ skewer and pour over the syrup, letting it █ sink in. Remove the cake from the tin on █ cool and cut into portions, serving with █ thick cream on the side.

TOP TIP

A toothpick is ideal for pricking the top of the cake before soaking in the syrup.

Coffee and Walnut Cake

SERVES 8

PREPARATION TIME 15 MINUTES

COOKING TIME 45 MINUTES

INGREDIENTS

150 g / 5 oz / 1 cup gluten-free self-raising flour, sifted

150 g / 5 oz / ⅔ cup butter, softened

150 g / 5 oz / ⅔ cup caster (superfine) sugar

3 medium eggs

4 tsp instant coffee granules

2 tbsp hot water

225 g / 8 oz / 2 cups walnuts

300 g / 10 ½ oz / 1 ⅓ cups unsalted butter, softened

250 g / 9 oz / 2 cups icing (confectioners') sugar, sifted

55 g / 2 oz / ⅓ cup dark chocolate chips

METHOD

- Preheat the oven to 180°C (160°C fan) / 350F / gas 4. Grease and line two 18 cm (7 in) cake tins with greaseproof paper.

- Combine the self-raising flour, butter, sugar and eggs in a large mixing bowl. Beat with an electric mixer for 2–3 minutes until smooth and creamy.

- Dissolve 2 tsp of the coffee granules in a little hot water to make a thin paste. Add to the batter and mix well to incorporate. Chop half of the walnuts and fold them through the batter.

- Divide the batter between the cake tins and bake for 25–30 minutes until risen. They are ready when a cake tester comes out clean from their centres when inserted.

- Remove to a wire rack to cool.

- Dissolve the remaining coffee granules in hot water and whisk into the butter and icing sugar in a mixing bowl.

- Once the sponges have cooled, turn them out from the tins and sit one on a cake stand. Spread the top with a third of the icing. Sandwich the other sponge on top and cover the entire cake with the remaining icing.

- Top with the remaining walnuts and the chocolate chips before slicing and serving.

TOP TIP

Level the top of the sponges with a serrated knife, if necessary.

Walnut and Orange Loaf

SERVES 8

PREPARATION TIME 15 MINUTES

COOKING TIME 1 HOUR 20 MINUTES

INGREDIENTS

175 g / 6 oz / 1 ¼ cups walnut flour, sifted

1 tsp bicarbonate of (baking) soda

a pinch of salt

110 g / 4 oz / ½ cup unsalted butter, softened

175 g / 6 oz / 1 cup soft light brown sugar

2 large eggs, beaten

½ tsp vanilla extract

2 very ripe large bananas, mashed

75 g / 3 oz / ¾ cup walnuts, finely chopped

2 oranges

125 g / 4 ½ oz / 1 cup icing (confectioners')
    sugar, sifted

METHOD

- Preheat the oven to 180°C (160°C fan) /
  350F / gas 4. Grease and line a 900 g /
  2 lb loaf tin with greaseproof paper.

- Combine the flour, bicarbonate
  of soda and salt in a mixing bowl.
  Cream together the butter and sugar
  in a separate mixing bowl.

- Beat in the egg and vanilla and then
  fold through the flour mixture in two
  additions until incorporated.

- Add the mashed banana and walnuts,
  mixing to incorporate. Scrape into the
  loaf tin and bake for 50–55 minutes
  until risen. A cake tester will come out
  clean from its centre.

- Remove to a wire rack to cool. Juice one
  of the oranges in a saucepan and whisk
  in the icing sugar. Cook over a medium
  heat until thick and syrupy.

- Slice the other orange and add to the
  syrup. Steep for 15 minutes.

- Prick the cake with a skewer and pour
  over the orange syrup, arranging the
  orange slices on top.

TOP TIP

Use hazelnuts (cobnuts)
and hazelnut flour for a
different nutty taste.

Hazelnut Meringue Cake

RVES 8

EPARATION TIME 15 MINUTES

OKING TIME 1 HOUR 20 MINUTES

GREDIENTS

arge egg whites

inch of salt

0 g / 7 oz / 1 cup caster (superfine) sugar

g / 3 oz / ¾ cup hazelnuts (cobnuts),
finely ground

0 ml / 9 fl. oz / 1 cup double (heavy) cream

5 g / 8 oz / 1 ½ cups raspberries

g / 2 ½ oz / ⅓ cup shelled pistachios,
crushed

g / 2 ½ oz / ½ cup icing (confectioners')
sugar

METHOD

- Preheat the oven to 140°C (120°C fan) /
  275F / gas 1. Grease and line two round
  baking trays with greaseproof paper.

- Beat the egg whites with a pinch of salt
  in a large, clean mixing bowl until
  softly peaked.

- Add half of the sugar and beat well
  until dissolved and smooth.

- Continue to beat in the remaining
  sugar, gradually, until the meringue is
  thick and glossy.

- Fold through the ground hazelnuts
  and spread the mixture into rounds on
  the baking trays.

- Bake for 1 hour 10–15 minutes until
  set and dry. Turn off the oven, open the
  door, and leave the meringues to cool
  in the oven.

- Beat the cream in a mixing bowl until
  softly peaked. Spread the cream over
  one of the meringues and top with the
  raspberries and pistachios.

- Sift over the icing sugar and top
  with the other round of meringue
  before serving.

TOP TIP

Rub a pinch of meringue
between your fingers;
if gritty, continue
beating.

Pecan Cupcakes

MAKES 24

PREPARATION TIME 15 MINUTES

COOKING TIME 20 MINUTES

INGREDIENTS

225 g / 8 oz / 2 cups pecan halves

150 g / 5 oz / 1 cup gluten-free plain
(all-purpose) flour

1 tsp gluten-free baking powder

¼ tsp bicarbonate of (baking) soda

¼ tsp salt

1 medium egg

175 g / 6 oz / 1 cup soft light brown sugar

2 tbsp whole milk

2 tbsp sunflower oil

1 tsp vanilla extract

1 ripe banana, mashed

225 g / 8 oz / 1 cup unsalted butter, softened

125 g / 4 ½ oz / 1 cup icing (confectioners')
sugar, sifted

75 g / 3 oz / ⅓ cup maple syrup

METHOD

- Preheat the oven to 190°C (170°C fan) /
  375F / gas 5 and line a 24-hole cupcake
  tin with cases. Set aside 24 pecan halves
  and finely chop the remainder.

- Sift together the flour, baking powder,
  bicarbonate of soda and salt into a
  mixing bowl.

- Whisk together the egg, sugar, milk,
  oil, vanilla, bananas and half of the
  chopped pecans.

- Stir into the flour mixture until just
  combined.

- Spoon into the paper cases and bake for
  15–18 minutes, until firm to the touch.
  Cool in the tins for 5 minutes, then
  place on a wire rack to cool completely.

- Beat together the butter and icing sugar
  in a mixing bowl until pale and thick.
  Stir in the maple syrup and remaining
  chopped pecans.

- Spoon into a piping bag and pipe swirls
  on top of the cakes. Place a pecan half
  on top of the buttercream before
  serving the cakes.

TOP TIP

Swirl 1–2 tbsp of maple
syrup into the batter
for a maple cupcake.

Victoria Sponge Cake

RVES 8

EPARATION TIME 25 MINUTES

OKING TIME 25 MINUTES

GREDIENTS

5 g / 8 oz / 1 cup caster (superfine) sugar

5 g / 8 oz / 1 cup margarine, softened

nedium eggs, beaten

5 g / 8 oz / 1 ½ cups gluten-free plain
  (all-purpose) flour, sifted

½ tsp gluten-free baking powder

0 ml / 9 fl. oz / 1 cup double (heavy) cream

sp vanilla extract

g / 2 ½ oz / ½ cup icing (confectioners')
  sugar

0 g / 9 oz / 1 cup raspberry jam (jelly)

METHOD

- Preheat the oven to 190°C (170°C fan) / 375F / gas 5.

- Grease and line two 20 cm (8 in) cake tins with greaseproof paper.

- Cream together the sugar and margarine in a mixing bowl until pale and fluffy; around 2–3 minutes.

- Beat in the eggs, one teaspoon at a time, until well incorporated. Fold in the flour and baking powder in three additions, mixing until smooth.

- Divide the batter between the prepared tins. Bake for 18–22 minutes until golden and risen. A toothpick should come out clean from their centres.

- Remove to a wire rack to cool.

- Whip the cream with the vanilla extract and icing sugar in mixing bowl until thick and peaked.

- Turn out the sponges and trim the top of one so that it is flat and even. Top with the cream, spreading it out evenly over the sponge.

- Top with the raspberry jam and sandwich the other sponge on top.

TOP TIP

Run a sharp knife around the insides of the cake tins to help loosen the sponges.

Basic White Bread

MAKES 1 LARGE LOAF

PREPARATION TIME 1 HOUR 45 MINUTES

COOKING TIME 50 MINUTES

INGREDIENTS

250 ml / 9 fl. oz / 1 cup milk, warmed to 43°C / 109F

55 g / 2 oz / ¼ cup caster (superfine) sugar

2 tsp dried active yeast

400 g / 14 oz / 2 ⅔ cups gluten-free plain (all-purpose) flour, sifted

1 tsp salt

55 g / 2 oz / ¼ cup unsalted butter, melted and cooled

2 medium eggs, beaten

METHOD

- Briefly whisk together the milk, sugar, and yeast in a mixing jug. Set to one side for 10 minutes.

- Combine the flour and salt in a large mixing bowl. Beat in the yeast mixture, gradually, until well combined.

- Beat in three-quarters of the butter and the eggs, continuing to mix for a further 2–3 minutes.

- Cover the bowl and leave it to rise in a warm place for 1 hour.

- Grease a 900 g / 2 lb loaf tin with the remaining butter. Stir the dough well and scrape into the prepared tin. Cover and leave to rise for a further 20 minutes in a warm place.

- Preheat the oven to 180°C (160°C fan) / 350F / gas 4.

- Bake the bread for 45–50 minutes until golden on top and risen.

- Remove the bread to a wire rack to cool completely. Turn out, slice, and serve when ready.

TOP TIP

An airing cupboard is ideal for proving the bread.

Wholemeal Loaf

KES 1 LARGE LOAF

PREPARATION TIME 1 HOUR 15 MINUTES

COOKING TIME 45 MINUTES

INGREDIENTS

- 0 ml / 10 ½ fl. oz / 1 ⅓ cups whole milk, warmed
- medium eggs, beaten
- sp white wine vinegar
- 0 g / 1 lb / 3 cups gluten-free wholemeal bread flour, plus extra for dusting
- bsp caster (superfine) sugar
- sp dried active yeast
- sp salt
- ml / 2 fl. oz / ¼ cup olive oil
- bsp gluten-free rolled oats

METHOD

- Briefly whisk together the milk, eggs and vinegar in a mixing jug.
- Combine the flour, sugar, yeast and salt in a large mixing bowl. Beat in the milk mixture, gradually, until well combined.
- Add the olive oil and continue to mix for a further 2 minutes. Turn out the dough onto a floured surface and knead briefly.
- Grease a 900 g / 2 lb loaf tin with a little olive oil. Shape the dough into the tin and leave to prove in a warm place for 1 hour. Preheat the oven to 180°C (160°C fan) / 350F / gas 4.
- Bake the bread for 40–45 minutes until golden on top and risen. Scatter the rolled oats over the loaf.
- Remove the bread to a wire rack to cool completely. Turn out, slice and serve when ready.

TOP TIP

Try using a gluten-free white bread flour instead of wholemeal.

Soda Bread

MAKES 1 LOAF

PREPARATION TIME 15 MINUTES

COOKING TIME 45 MINUTES

INGREDIENTS

100 g / 3 ½ oz / ⅔ cup rice flour, sifted
100 g / 3 ½ oz / ⅔ cup gluten-free plain
    (all-purpose) flour, sifted
75 g / 3 oz / ½ cup potato flour, plus extra
    for dusting
75 g / 3 oz / ½ cup cornflour (cornstarch)
2 tsp Xanthan gum
2 tbsp caster (superfine) sugar
½ tsp salt
½ tsp bicarbonate of (baking) soda
½ tsp cream of tartar
55 g / 2 oz / ¼ cup unsalted butter, cubed
1 large egg, beaten
110 g / 4 oz / ½ cup buttermilk

METHOD

- Combine the flours, cornflour, Xanthan gum, sugar, salt, bicarbonate of soda and cream of tartar in a mixing bowl. Whisk briefly to mix.

- Preheat the oven to 190°C (170°C fan) / 375F / gas 5. Line a large baking tray with greaseproof paper.

- Rub the butter into the flour mixture until it resembles breadcrumbs. Add the egg and buttermilk, stirring until a dough comes together.

- Knead the dough briefly, then shape into an oval. Lift onto the baking tray and score the top with a sharp knife. Dust with potato flour.

- Bake for 40–45 minutes until golden and firm to the touch.

- Remove to a wire rack to cool.

TOP TIP

Add a handful of raisins to the dough for a fruity soda bread.

Sun-dried Tomato Bread

MAKES 1 LARGE LOAF

PREPARATION TIME 1 HOUR 50 MINUTES

COOKING TIME 50 MINUTES

INGREDIENTS

- ml / 9 fl. oz / 1 cup milk, warmed to 43°C / 109F
- g / 2 oz / ¼ cup caster (superfine) sugar
- p dried active yeast
- g / 14 oz / 2 ⅔ cups gluten-free plain (all-purpose) flour, sifted
- p salt
- g / 2 oz / ¼ cup unsalted butter, melted and cooled
- medium eggs, beaten
- g / 5 oz / 1 cup sun-dried tomatoes in oil, drained and chopped
- g / 5 oz / 1 cup pitted black olives, sliced
- g / 5 oz / 1 ½ cups mozzarella, cubed
- g / 3 oz / ¾ cup pumpkin seeds
- g / 2 oz / ½ cup sunflower seeds

METHOD

- Briefly whisk together the milk, sugar and yeast in a mixing jug. Set to one side for 10 minutes.

- Combine the flour and salt in a large mixing bowl. Gradually beat in the yeast mixture until well combined.

- Beat in three-quarters of the butter and the eggs, and continue to mix for a further 2–3 minutes. Add the sun-dried tomato, olives, and mozzarella to the dough, mixing well.

- Cover the bowl and leave it to rise in a warm place for 1 hour.

- Grease a 900 g / 2 lb loaf tin with the remaining butter. Stir the dough well and scrape into the prepared tin. Cover and leave to rise for a further 20 minutes in a warm place.

- Preheat the oven to 180°C (160°C fan) / 350F / gas 4. Top the dough with the pumpkin and sunflower seeds.

- Bake the bread for 45–50 minutes until golden on top and risen.

- Remove the bread to a wire rack to cool completely. Turn out, slice, and serve when ready.

TOP TIP

For dairy-free, replace the butter with margarine and omit the mozzarella.

Fruit Bread

METHOD

- Briefly whisk together the milk, sugar and yeast in a mixing jug. Set to one side for 10 minutes.

- Combine the flour and salt in a large mixing bowl. Beat in the yeast mixture, gradually, until well combined.

- Beat in half of the butter and then the eggs, mixing for a further 2–3 minutes. Mix in the raisins.

- Cover the bowl and leave it to rise in a warm place for 1 hour.

- Grease a 900 g / 2 lb loaf tin with 1 tbsp of the remaining butter. Stir the dough well and scrape into the prepared tin. Cover and leave to rise for a further 20 minutes in a warm place.

- Preheat the oven to 180°C (160°C fan) / 350F / gas 4. Score the top of the bread in a rough diamond pattern. Bake the bread for 45–50 minutes until golden on top and risen.

- Remove the bread to a wire rack and brush the top with the remaining melted butter. Leave to cool before serving.

MAKES 1 LOAF
PREPARATION TIME 1 HOUR 50 MINUTES
COOKING TIME 50 MINUTES

INGREDIENTS

250 ml / 9 fl. oz / 1 cup milk, warmed to 43°C / 109F

55 g / 2 oz / ¼ cup caster (superfine) sugar

2 tsp dried active yeast

400 g / 14 oz / 2 ⅔ cups gluten-free plain (all-purpose) flour, sifted

1 tsp salt

55 g / 2 oz / ¼ cup unsalted butter, melted and cooled

2 medium eggs, beaten

150 g / 5 oz / 1 cup raisins

TOP TIP

2 tbsp of mixed citrus peel adds a pleasing tang to this bread.

DESSERTS AND
SWEET TREATS

DESSERTS AND SWEET TREATS

Cherry Clafoutis

SERVES 4

PREPARATION TIME 25 MINUTES

COOKING TIME 50 MINUTES

INGREDIENTS

400 g / 14 oz / 2 cups canned cherries, drained

2 tbsp kirsch

2 tbsp caster (superfine) sugar

55 g / 2 oz / ¼ cup unsalted butter

4 small eggs

75 g / 3 oz / ⅓ cup golden caster (superfine) sugar

1 tsp vanilla extract

55 g / 2 oz / ⅓ cup cornflour (cornstarch)

250 ml / 9 fl. oz / 1 cup whole milk

2 tbsp granulated sugar

METHOD

- Preheat the oven to 180°C (160°C fan) / 350F / gas 4.

- Toss the cherries with the kirsch and caster sugar in a large mixing bowl. Set to one side for 15 minutes.

- Melt the butter in a saucepan until brown and nutty in aroma. Remove from the heat and leave to cool.

- Whisk together the eggs, golden caster sugar and vanilla extract until smooth and creamy. Add the cornflour, and whisk well until smooth.

- Whisk in the butter and milk until evenly incorporated.

- Arrange most of the cherries in a 900 g / 2 lb oval baking dish. Pour over the batter and arrange the remaining cherries on top.

- Bake for 35–40 minutes until a tester comes out clean from the centre.

- Remove to a wire rack, sprinkle with granulated sugar, and allow the pudding to cool for 5 minutes before serving.

TOP TIP
Reserve the syrup or juice from the cherries and use as a garnish.

Redcurrant Cheesecake

SERVES 8

PREPARATION TIME 15 MINUTES

COOKING TIME 2 HOURS 45 MINUTES

INGREDIENTS

- 100 g / 4 oz / 1 cup ground almonds
- 100 g / 4 oz / ⅔ cup rice flour
- 50 g / 2 oz / ⅓ cup soft light brown sugar
- 75 g / 3 oz / ⅓ cup butter, melted
- 600 g / 1 lb 5 oz / 3 cups cream cheese, softened
- 300 g / 10 ½ oz / 1 ⅓ cups caster (superfine) sugar
- 150 g / 5 oz / ⅔ cup sour cream
- 3 large eggs, beaten
- 1 tbsp lemon juice
- 1 tsp vanilla extract
- 300 g / 10 ½ oz / 1 ½ cups frozen redcurrants
- 75 g / 2 ½ oz / ½ cup icing (confectioners') sugar, sifted

METHOD

- Pulse together the ground almonds, rice flour, brown sugar and butter in a food processor until combined.
- Pack the mixture into the base of a 23 cm (9 in) springform cake tin, spreading it evenly with the back of a tablespoon. Chill until ready to use.
- Preheat the oven to 190°C (170°C fan) / 375F / gas 5.
- Beat together the cream cheese, caster sugar, sour cream, eggs, lemon juice and vanilla extract for 3–4 minutes, until smooth.
- Pour the mixture onto the chilled crust, tapping the tin lightly to release any trapped air bubbles. Line a roasting tray with a tea towel. Lift the tin into the tray, and pour boiling water around the tin so that it comes halfway up its side.
- Bake for 30 minutes. Reduce the oven to 120°C (100°C fan) / 250F / gas ½ and bake the cheesecake for 2 hours until set.
- Remove to a wire rack to cool. Cook the redcurrants and icing sugar with 2 tbsp of water in a saucepan set over a medium heat.
- Cook until soft and juicy, stirring frequently. Remove from the heat and leave to cool. Spoon over the cheesecake before serving.

TOP TIP

This cheesecake can be topped with any kind of berries; try raspberries or blueberries.

Crème Brûlée

SERVES 4

PREPARATION TIME 4 HOURS 25 MINUTES

COOKING TIME 2 HOURS

INGREDIENTS

500 ml / 18 fl. oz / 2 cups whole milk

500 ml / 18 fl. oz / 2 cups double (heavy) cream

1 vanilla pod, split in half with seeds scraped out

6 large egg yolks

110 g / 4 oz / ½ cup caster (superfine) sugar

75 g / 3 oz / ½ cup soft light brown sugar

METHOD

- Preheat the oven to 120°C (100°C fan) / 250F / gas ½.

- Warm together the milk, cream and split vanilla pod in a saucepan set over a moderate heat until simmering.

- Whisk together the egg yolks and caster sugar in a large mixing bowl until pale and thick.

- Gradually whisk in the milk and cream mixture until incorporated. Line a roasting tray with a tea towel and arrange four individual heatproof ramekins on top of the towel.

- Strain the custard mixture into a jug. Pour boiling water into the tin so that it comes halfway up the outsides of the ramekins, and then divide the mixture between the ramekins.

- Transfer the roasting tin to the oven to cook for 1 hour 30–45 minutes until just set. They will be ready when they are firm with a slight wobble when tapped.

- Remove to a wire rack and allow the custards to cool slightly before chilling for 4 hours.

- When ready to serve, sprinkle the tops of the custards with brown sugar and caramelise using a chef's blowtorch.

TOP TIP

Use 1 tsp of pure vanilla extract in a pinch if you don't have a vanilla pod.

Cinnamon Pear Tart

SERVES 4

PREPARATION TIME 25 MINUTES

COOKING TIME 45 MINUTES

INGREDIENTS

- 250 g / 9 oz ready-made gluten-free shortcrust pastry
- A little gluten-free plain (all-purpose) flour, for dusting
- 2 tbsp butter, softened
- 150 g / 5 oz / 1 ½ cups ground almonds
- 150 g / 5 oz / ⅔ cup caster (superfine) sugar
- 55 g / 2 oz / ⅓ cup cocoa powder, sifted
- 2 large eggs
- 1 tsp vanilla extract
- ½ tsp ground cinnamon
- 8 canned pear halves, drained
- 2 tbsp icing (confectioners') sugar

METHOD

- Preheat the oven to 180°C (160°C fan) / 350F / gas 4. Roll out the pastry on a lightly floured surface into a round approximately 30 cm (12 in) round and ½ cm (¼ in) thick.

- Use the round of pastry to line the base and sides of a 20 cm (8 in) fluted tart tin. Trim away the excess pastry and prick the base with a fork, and chill until ready to fill.

- Blend together the butter, ground almonds, sugar, cocoa powder, eggs, vanilla extract and ground cinnamon in a food processor. Once smooth, scrape into the lined pastry case.

- Place the pear halves in the filling and bake the tart for 40–45 minutes until the pastry is golden and cooked and the filling is set.

- Remove to a wire rack to cool. Dust with icing sugar before serving.

TOP TIP

Canned peach halves make for a nice alternative to pears.

Berry Sorbet

METHOD

- Combine the water, berries and sugar in a saucepan and cook over a medium heat until softened.

- Blend the mixture in a food processor until smooth. Pass it through a sieve into the bowl of an ice cream machine.

- Churn the mixture in the ice cream machine according to the manufacturer's instructions until frozen and set. Cover and freeze for 2 hours.

- Remove the sorbet from the freezer 10 minutes before serving. Scoop into martini glasses and serve.

SERVES 4

PREPARATION TIME 2 HOURS 10 MINUTES

COOKING TIME 15 MINUTES

INGREDIENTS

250 ml / 9 fl. oz / 1 cup water
400 g / 14 oz / 2 ½ cups frozen mixed berries
100 g / 3 ½ oz / ½ cup caster (superfine) sugar

TOP TIP

Warm an ice cream scoop in hot water for perfect scoops each time.

Fruit Rice Pudding

SERVES 4

PREPARATION TIME 10 MINUTES

COOKING TIME 45 MINUTES

INGREDIENTS

1 l / 1 pint 16 fl. oz / 4 cups whole milk
75 g / 3 oz / ⅓ cup caster (superfine) sugar
1 tsp vanilla extract
200 g / 7 oz / 1 cup pudding rice
4 tbsp double (heavy) cream
pinch of nutmeg
300 g / 10 ½ oz / 2 cups raspberries
4 ripe figs, sliced
75 g / 2 ½ oz / ½ cup icing (confectioners')
   sugar
½ lemon, juiced

METHOD

- Combine the milk, caster sugar and vanilla extract in a saucepan. Cook over a moderate heat until boiling and then reduce to a low heat.

- Add the rice, stir well and continue to cook over a low heat, stirring frequently, until the rice has absorbed the milk and is tender; 25–30 minutes.

- Once the rice is tender and has absorbed most of the milk, stir through the cream and nutmeg. Keep warm over a low heat.

- Combine the raspberries, figs, icing sugar, lemon juice, and 2 tbsp of water in a saucepan. Cook over a medium heat, stirring occasionally, until softened, juicy and syrupy.

- Spoon the rice pudding into glasses and top with the fruit compote before serving.

TOP TIP
Experiment with different kinds of rice, such as short-grain and Arborio.

Dark Chocolate Soufflés

SERVES 4

PREPARATION TIME 15 MINUTES

COOKING TIME 40 MINUTES

INGREDIENTS

75 g / 3 oz / ⅓ cup unsalted butter, softened
55 g / 2 oz / ⅓ cup gluten-free plain
   (all-purpose) flour, sifted
300 ml / 10 ½ fl. oz / 1 ⅓ cups whole milk
125 g / 4 ½ oz / ¾ cup dark chocolate, grated
55 g / 2 oz / ¼ cup caster (superfine) sugar
3 medium egg yolks
4 medium egg whites
a pinch of salt
2 tbsp icing (confectioners') sugar
2 tbsp white chocolate chips

METHOD

- Preheat the oven to 190°C (170°C fan) / 375F / gas 5. Grease four heatproof teacups with a little softened butter. Chill until ready to use.

- Melt the remaining butter in a saucepan set over a medium heat. Whisk in the flour and cook for 1 minute, whisking, until thickened.

- Whisk in the milk and cook until thickened, 2 minutes. Stir in the chocolate and 2 tbsp of the caster sugar. Remove the saucepan from the heat and beat in the egg yolks.

- Beat the egg whites with a pinch of salt until stiffly peaked. Add the remaining sugar and beat until thick and glossy.

- Stir one third of the beaten egg white into the chocolate mixture. Fold in the rest using a rubber spatula and divide the batter between the buttered teacups.

- Sit the cups on a baking tray and transfer the tray to the oven. Bake for 22–25 minutes until the soufflés are coming away from the edge of the cups.

- Remove from the oven and serve with a dusting of icing sugar and a few white chocolate chips on top.

TOP TIP
Beat the egg whites in a clean, oil-free bowl for best results.

Baked Chocolate Mousse

SERVES 4

PREPARATION TIME 20 MINUTES

COOKING TIME 40 MINUTES

INGREDIENTS

- 100 ml / 4 fl. oz / ½ cup water
- 50 g / 2 oz / ⅓ cup cocoa powder, plus extra for dusting
- 1 tsp instant coffee granules
- 150 g / 5 oz / 1 cup dark chocolate, grated
- 4 tbsp brandy
- 2 large eggs
- 2 large egg whites
- 75 g / 3 oz / ⅓ cup caster (superfine) sugar
- 1 pinch of salt

METHOD

- Preheat the oven to 180°C (160°C fan) / 350F / gas 4.
- Place the water in a saucepan and heat until boiling. Whisk in the cocoa powder and coffee granules until smooth.
- Gently whisk in the chocolate, off the heat, and then stir in the brandy. Leave to cool for 10 minutes.
- Combine the eggs, egg whites, sugar and salt in a heatproof bowl set over a saucepan of half-filled simmering water.
- Cook the mixture, whisking constantly, until it registers 115°C / 239F. Remove the bowl from the heat and continue to beat for 4–5 minutes until the mixture leaves a ribbon-like trail on the surface.
- Stir one third of the egg mixture into the chocolate mixture. Fold the chocolate mixture into the remaining egg mixture with a rubber spatula.
- Divide the mixture between four individual ceramic ramekins and place on a baking tray. Bake for 22–25 minutes until set.
- Remove to a wire rack to cool. Cover and chill overnight before serving with a dusting of cocoa powder.

TOP TIP

Remove the brandy for an alcohol-free version.

Chocolate Chip Cookies

MAKES 12

PREPARATION TIME 30 MINUTES

COOKING TIME 15 MINUTES

INGREDIENTS

225 g / 8 oz / 1 ½ cups gluten-free plain
   (all-purpose) flour, sifted

110 g / 4 oz / ½ cup caster (superfine) sugar

½ tsp salt

150 g / 5 oz / ⅔ cup butter, melted and cooled

110 g / 4 oz / ⅔ cup dark chocolate chips

2 medium eggs, beaten

½ tsp vanilla extract

1 l / 1 pint 16 fl. oz / 4 cups milk, to serve

2 tbsp chocolate syrup, to serve

METHOD

- Mix together the flour, sugar and salt in a large mixing bowl.

- Beat in the melted butter until the mixture starts to come together.

- Add the dark chocolate chips, eggs and vanilla extract. Mix until a stiff cookie dough forms, then cover and chill for 15 minutes.

- Grease and line two baking trays with greaseproof paper. Preheat the oven to 180°C (160°C fan) / 350F / gas 4.

- Take generous tablespoons of the chilled dough and drop onto the sheets, spaced apart.

- Press down lightly and bake for 12–15 minutes until just set and starting to brown.

- Remove to wire racks to cool before serving with glasses of cold milk and the chocolate syrup to mix.

TOP TIP
Let them bake for 3 minutes extra for firmer, crunchier cookies.

Chocolate Muffins

KES 12

EPARATION TIME 15 MINUTES

OKING TIME 30 MINUTES

REDIENTS

- g / 9 oz / 1 ⅔ cups gluten-free plain (all-purpose) flour
- g / 2 oz / ⅓ cup cocoa powder
- p gluten-free baking powder
- rge eggs
- g / 4 oz / ½ cup golden caster (superfine) sugar
- ml / 2 fl. oz / ¼ cup vegetable oil
- ml / 8 fl. oz / 1 cup whole milk
- p vanilla extract
- g / 3 ½ oz / ⅔ cup chocolate chips
- sp icing (confectioners') sugar

METHOD

- Preheat the oven to 180°C (160°C fan) / 350F / gas 4 and line a 12-hole muffin tray with cases.

- Stir together the flour, cocoa powder and baking powder in a mixing bowl.

- Combine the eggs, caster sugar, oil, milk and vanilla extract in a large jug and whisk until combined.

- Pour into the dry ingredients and stir until just combined. Stir the chocolate chips into the batter.

- Divide the batter between the cases and bake for 20–25 minutes until set and starting to crack on top. Test with a wooden toothpick, if it comes out clean, the muffins are done.

- Remove the muffins to a wire rack to cool, then dust with icing sugar before serving.

TOP TIP

Make sure that the muffin batter isn't overmixed for best results.

Brownies

MAKES 12

PREPARATION TIME 10 MINUTES

COOKING TIME 50 MINUTES

INGREDIENTS

350 g / 12 oz / 2 ⅓ cups dark chocolate, chopped
225 g / 8 oz / 1 cup unsalted butter, softened
3 large eggs
250 g / 9 oz / 1 ⅓ cups soft light brown sugar
125 g / 4 ½ oz / ¾ cup gluten-free plain
    (all-purpose) flour
1 tsp gluten-free baking powder
a pinch of salt

METHOD

- Preheat the oven to 170°C (150°C fan) / 325F / gas 3. Grease and line an 18 cm (7 in) square baking tin with greaseproof paper.

- Melt together the chocolate and butter in a saucepan set over a medium heat, stirring occasionally until smooth.

- Remove from the heat and allow to cool a little.

- In a large mixing bowl, whisk the eggs until thick and whisk in the sugar until thick and glossy.

- Beat in the melted chocolate mixture, and then fold in the flour, baking powder and salt until incorporated.

- Pour into the baking tray and tap lightly a few times to release any trapped air bubbles.

- Bake for 35–40 minutes until the surface has set; test with a wooden toothpick, if it comes out almost clean, the brownie is done.

- Remove to a wire rack to cool before turning out, slicing, and serving.

TOP TIP

A large handful of chopped walnuts will lend a crunchy texture.

Lemon Shortbread Biscuits

MAKES 24–28

PREPARATION TIME 1 HOUR 20 MINUTES

COOKING TIME 15 MINUTES

INGREDIENTS

200 g / 7 oz / 1 ¾ cups gluten-free plain (all-purpose) flour, plus extra for dusting

100 g / 3 ½ oz / ¾ cup ground almonds

200 g / 7 oz / 1 cup butter, softened

125 g / 4 ½ oz / 1 cup icing (confectioners') sugar

1 tbsp caster (superfine) sugar, plus extra for dusting

1 tsp vanilla extract

2 medium egg yolks

150 g / 5 oz / ⅔ cup lemon curd

METHOD

- Mix together the flour and ground almonds.

- Whisk together the butter, icing sugar, caster sugar, vanilla and egg yolks until blended. Stir in the flour mixture until smooth. Wrap in cling film and chill for 1 hour.

- Preheat the oven to 170°C (150°C fan) / 325F / gas 3. Line two large baking trays with greaseproof paper.

- Knead the dough lightly on a floured surface and roll out to ½ cm (¼ in) thickness. Use a fluted cutter to cut out rounds and re-roll the trimmings.

- Arrange the rounds on the baking trays and cut out small holes from the centres of half of the rounds.

- Bake for 10–12 minutes until pale golden. Cool on the trays for 5 minutes, then place on a wire rack to cool completely.

- Spread the lemon curd on the rounds without holes and place the cut-out rounds on top, pressing gently. Sprinkle with caster sugar before serving.

TOP TIP

Re-roll the trimmings gently to keep the light texture of the shortbread.

Macaroons

MAKES 24

PREPARATION TIME 30 MINUTES

COOKING TIME 30 MINUTES

INGREDIENTS

750 g / 1 lb 10 oz / 6 cups icing (confectioners')
    sugar, sifted
350 g / 12 oz / 3 cups ground almonds
4 medium egg whites
pinch of salt
natural food dye, assorted shades
150 ml / 5 fl. oz / ⅔ cup double
    (heavy) cream
150 g / 5 oz / 1 cup dark chocolate, chopped
350 g / 12 oz / 1 ½ cups unsalted butter,
    softened
65 g / 2 ½ oz / ½ cups shelled pistachios
100 g / 3 ½ oz / ½ cup strawberry jam (jelly)

METHOD

- Preheat the oven to 180°C (160°C fan) / 3
  / gas 4. Grease and line two large baking
  trays with greaseproof paper.

- Combine 450 g / 1 lb / 4 ½ cups of icing s
  with the ground almonds in a mixing bo

- Beat the egg whites with a pinch of salt in
  separate mixing bowl until stiffly peaked
  Fold the egg whites into the almond mix
  and divide between four small bowls.

- Dye the mixtures with the assorted food
  dyes, mixing thoroughly, then spoon the
  macaroon mixture into separate piping b
  fitted with round nozzles. Pipe 12 round
  each onto the baking trays, spaced apart.

- Leave them to set for 15 minutes, then ba
  for 8–10 minutes until just set. Remove to
  wire rack to cool.

- Heat the cream in a heatproof bowl in the
  microwave until hot, then add the choco
  and stir until smooth. Beat together the
  butter and icing sugar in a mixing bowl
  using an electric mixer. Once pale and th
  divide the mixture between two bowls.

- Blitz the pistachios in a food processor u
  finely ground, then add to one bowl, stir
  well to incorporate. Spoon the buttercrea
  and jam into separate piping bags.

- Pipe the buttercreams and jam onto the
  underside of the macaroons, sandwiching
  them against the other macaroon halves
  to complete.

TOP TIP

Try using ground
hazelnuts (cobnuts)
instead of ground
almonds.

INDEX